SRI AMARNATHA CAVE
The Abode of Shiva

SRI AMARNATHA CAVE

THE ABODE OF SHIVA

by

F.M. Hassnain, Yoshiaki Miura, Vijay Pandita

Foreword by

Dr. Karan Singh

NIRMAL PUBLISHERS & DISTRIBUTORS
B-2, Vishal Enclave, Najafgarh Road,
New Delhi-110027
Phone : 5413460

Published by
Nirmal Publishers & Distributors
B-2, Vishal Enclave, Najafgarh Road,
New Delhi-110027
Phone : 5413460

Printed at
Hardev Printers
A-49/1, Mayapuri, Phase-I
New Delhi-110064

CONTENTS

MANSAROVAR
3, NYAYA MARG
CHANAKYAPURI
NEW DELHI-110021
Tel. 3011744

Dr KARAN SINGH

Foreword

The immortal cave of Śri Amareshwara in Kashmir, known as the Amarnath Cave, is invested with many sacred and mysterious phenomena. Here emerges the ice-Lingam of Shiva on the full moon, Puranmashi, and its darshan is breath-taking. During summer thousands of pilgrims visit the Cave. They often see two white pigeons come out of it, and for the devotees these two birds represent the Creator of this universe, Shiva and his consort, Parvati. Since times immemorial, pilgrims from various parts of the country and recently from abroad have been visiting this sacred abode of Shiva.

I am happy to learn that the ancient Mahatmya Amareshwara has been translated by eminent scholars like Prof. Fida M. Hassnain, Prof. Y. Muira of Fujita University, Japan, and Mrs. Vijay Pandita of the Kashmir Council of Historical & Cultural Research. It is a welcome coincidence that mystery about this Holy Cave is being unveiled by Prof. Hassnain, who is a Muslim. Prof. Muira, who is a Buddhist and Mrs. Pandita, who is a Hindu. While congratulating them, I have to record that this sacred Cave has among its guardians a Muslim family from Anantnag, Kashmir, who receives his share of offerings made at the Holy Cave every year. I am sure this book will be read out with great interest.

Karan Singh

(KARAN SINGH)

Introduction

Each year, in the month of Shravan (July-August) when the moon is full, thousands of devotees of Lord Shiva and his consort Parvati, gather in front of the famous cave of Sri Amarnatha, situated in the picturesque Pahalgam in Kashmir. This sacred cave enshrines a naturally formed ice Lingam, the symbol of Shiva, which waxes and wanes with the moon. This sacred Lingam reaches its full length on the full moon night, which is fixed as the time of darshan for the pilgrims.

According to an ancient tradition, it is in this cave that Shiva explained the secret of salvation to his consort. As such, this sacred cave has been termed as the abode of Shiva. When the god and the goddess were in the penultimate position of ananda thandava, two servants of the Lord, overheard these secrets and, were converted into two pigeons, which are seen every year by the pilgrims, flying near the cave.

The talk between Lord Shiva and his divine consort Parvati, is preserved for us in the ancient Sanskrit manuscript, entitled: Amareshvara Mahatmya. We have made this rare manuscript the base of our book, by translating it and editing it in our own style. In this work, we were helped with material as well as useful suggestions by Prof. S.L. Vaishnavi, Prof. N.K. Gurtoo, Pandit P.N. Raina, Pandit J.N. Ganhar and Mr. Mohammad Amin Pandit. For photographs, we are indebted to the Photo Officer, Information Department, Curator, S.P.S. Museum and M/s. Lica Studios, Srinagar. We acknowledge with gratitude the help we obtained from the sources cited in this work. We are indebted to the concerned authors as well as publishers.

F.M. Hassnain
Yoshiaki Miura
Vijay Pandita

March, 1987

Introduction

Each year in the month of Shravan (July-August) when the moon is full, thousands of devotees of Lord Shiva and his consort Parvati gather in front of the famous cave of Sri Amarnath situated in the picturesque Pahalgam in Kashmir. The sacred cave enshrines a naturally formed ice Lingam, the symbol of Shiva, which waxes and wanes with the moon. This sacred Lingam reaches its full length on the full moon night which is fixed as the date of darsan for the pilgrims.

According to an ancient tradition, it is in this cave that Shiva explained the secret of salvation to his consort. As such this sacred cave has been treated as the abode of Shiva. When the god and the goddess were in the conjugate position, [illegible] Chandeva, two servants of the Lord, overheard these secrets and were converted into two pigeons, which are seen every year by the pilgrims, living near the cave.

The talk between Lord Shiva and his divine consort Parvati is preserved for us in the ancient Sanskrit manuscript, entitled Amareshvara Mahatmya. We have made this rare manuscript the basis of our book, by translating it and editing it in our own style. In this work we are helped with material as well as useful suggestions by Prof. S.L. Vaishnavi, Prof. N.K. Ganjoo, Pandit P.N. Raina, Pandit J.C. Ganjoo and Mr. Mohammad Amin Pandit. For photographs, we are indebted to the Photo Office, Information Department, Curator, S.P.S. Museum and M.S. Library, Srinagar. We acknowledge with gratitude the help we obtained from the sources cited in this work. We are indebted to the concerned authors as well as publishers.

F.M. HASSNAIN
YOSHIAKI MIURA
VIJAY PANDITA

March 1987

CHAPTER I

The Abode of Shiva

She who is Shiva in Shiva-kund,
She who is Shakti in Shakti-kund,
She who is Sat, Chit and Anand,
To thee who are beloved I bow down.

One cannot say what the Absolute is like; one can only say what it is not. As the Absolute can never be the object of perception, none can enumerate its qualities. At the same time our thought and speech turn eagerly to search the Absolute which takes forms to favour the devotees. This Absolute is divided for us, into three bodies namely, Brahma, Vishnu and Shiva. As such this Divinity is described in the scriptures as the creator, the preserver and the destroyer. There are different paths of realization but the Absolute reveals itself of its own accord. With Rajas in the form of Brahma he creates, with Sattva in the form of Vishnu he preserves, and with Tamas in the form of Rudra he destroys. He is Shiva the Three-eyed One, who drank poison as an act of favour to gods and demons, to save the world from destruction.

This universe with all its infinite variety of objects is nothing but a manifestation of Shiva himself. This very aspect of his manifestation is known as Shakti, who is the creative power behind him. She has a number of moods and it is all due to her that Shiva is able to manifest himself.

She is Shiva in the Shiva-kund,
She is Shakti in the Shakti-kund,
She is the embodiment of Sat, Chit and Anand,
We bow before her.

We adore thee!
O Divine Mother!
The consort of Shiva,
Who reveals in the sport of protecting the universe;
For whose acts of creation and destruction:
The supreme Lord Shiva:
Is the witness.

Then said Shiva to Brahma and Vishnu:

I am the creator of the world,
I am the preserver of the world, and
I am the destroyer of the world.

Whatever you see in the cosmos, it is all due to me, it all belongs to me.

I am the sun;
I am the moon;
I am the fire;
I am the air;
I am the water;
I am the space;
I am the earth;
I am the self;
I am the God.

As I am formless, so is Lingam. That is the reason that humanity worships me through the Lingam. See my advent in the form of the Lingam!

After having uttered the above words of wisdom, Shiva disappeared from the scene.

Sutta has said that the worship of the Lingam will enable humanity to get released from the bondage of actions while enjoying the blessings of earthly life. The Lingam is to be made of the heavenly stone, the meteorite, or the sacred metal and iron dug out of the earth. Its length should be nearly eleven or twelve fingers. The Lingam is to be worshipped every day, so that merit is gained by the devotee. Worship of the Lingam at dawn results in the attainment of every wish; while the night worship gives contentment and happiness.

Worship offered to the Lingam helps the devotee to get desirable objects. Such worship is to be done at sacred places, such as, river banks, caves, mountain tops, sources of water, forest, gardens and temples. The Devi was born first as Sati and then as Parvati. As such, the Devi feels satisfied when the Yoni is also worshipped along with the Lingam.[1]

The union between Shiva and Shakti is manifest in Lingam. Shiva gets pleased to see devotees worshipping his Lingam.

O Three-eyed One, my salutations to Thee!
O Giver of boons, my salutations to Thee!
O Giver of refuge, my salutations to Thee!
O God of the gods, my salutations to Thee!

Words of Wisdom

When requested to bestow the words of wisdom, Sutta said: Sin should be detested at every time and at every place. Your work, your thinking, your action, all your life should be free from sin. By gaining knowledge, one can conquer sin. One can lead a purposeful life by remaining away from sin.

It is the duty of the people belonging to the four castes—Brahmans, Khastriyas, Vaishas and the Shudaras—to keep God in their mind, from morning till night. Then they should think of their every-day work. Face the East and meditate: this is sure to give you success. It is better to take a bath in a stream of running water. One should sit in water; pour out water with his hands to the sun, while reciting mantaras.

All six days of the week are attributes of the six Devas. It is your duty to please these Devas by recitation, meditation, offerings and prayers. If you desire to be rich, pray on Monday. It you wish to be healthy, pray on Tuesday. If you desire to have children, pray on Wednesday. If you want to live long, pray on Thursday. Your other wishes can be fulfilled on Friday.

1. Shiva-Maha-Purana.

If you aspire for love, then perform necessary rituals on Saturday. In the same way sins can be forgiven on Sunday.

The Brahmans can pray with the help of mantaras, the Shudaras can take recourse to tantaras; but if you have no wealth to offer to the gods, then make them pleased with your meditation.

In order to realize the Atman, it is necessary to employ the following means:

(1) Puja, which means worship.
(2) Japa, which means recitation of mantaras, hymns and meditation.

For Puja, an object is used, such as an image, Lingam and Yoni or Yantra. The image or idol is the representation of the Deity.

The supreme controller of the universe is all-doing, all knowing, all-sustaining and infinite. On the emergence of desire at the creational stage. He evolves, out of His own Self, the octad *Vijinana-kevala*. He assigns to them the functions of sustenance, destruction, preservation and benefaction. For their sphere of action He manifested seven crores of mantaras with their respective ranges. The Self comes into manifestation in four-fold capacity as Shiva, mantramahesha, mantresha and mantra.[1]

Worship of Idols

Worship of idols made from earth can fulfil all your wishes. It is better to obtain pure and clean silt from a stream or a spring, which should be mixed with perfume and milk. Then an idol of any god or goddess should be moulded out of this material. If it is proposed to make a Lingam out of it, then it can be done by any Brahman. If you desire to save yourself from future births, then it is proper for you to worship the Lingam of Shiva. You must think that Yoni and Lingam are just like your mother and father and their unity manifests Shiva. Just as Nature and Man, the Lingam of Shiva is the

1. Malini-vijay-ottara-tantra.

creator. Man creates a man but the man gets himself netted in desire, with the result that the soul goes out, resulting in the death of a human being. Then a cycle of births and re-births rotates. If you want to check your re-birth then, offer prayers to the Lingam, which created you. God is the bestower of this phalus, so it is better to worship God in the shape of Shiv-Ling. The Lingam describes the meeting of Shiva with Shakti and Shiva gets very much pleased if his Lingam is worshipped by devotees. It is essential to wash the idol with a mixture of honey, milk, butter, urine of a cow. After it, the idol be again washed with milk. Then, sugar cane, and cow milk be offered to the idol. Any one who worships the Shiva-Lingam in this way, he saves himself from re-births.[1]

It must be kept in mind that the idol is the representation of the invisible Supreme. As God or the gods and goddesses are invoked in the idols, these are holy and sacred.

> Those who think themselves to be different from the Lord will never see him. Meditate upon yourself as the Deity, with your mind. By meditating upon a Deva, one becomes Deva and by meditating upon a Devi, one becomes Devi. To know God is to be God, for He is known by being God. This is the essence of Shiva worship, which should be done by meditation, recitation of hymns and offerings.

The Story of Parvati

The king of the Himalayas married a princess named Manika. The queen was a pious lady and spent her time in prayers and meditation. She gave birth to a lovely girl, who was named Parvati by the king. At the time of her birth all the gods came to congratulate the queen. The astrologers predicted that the maiden would be married to a mendicant. Her parents became sad to hear all this but reconciled.

When Parvati became a maiden, her mother thought of marrying her with a prince of equal rank. But she loved Shiva

1. Shiva-Maha-Purana; Partheau Pojan, pp. 26-28.

from her early childhood and wanted to marry him at any cost. She was told that Shiva had left his house and lived in a cave. He lived in the company of goblins, naked like a mendicant. He is a beggar and lives on charity of others. Having no house, he roams from place to place in the company of bad characters. Hearing all this, Parvati declared that come what may, she would marry no other person than this very beggar—Shiva.[1]

While Parvati burned in the love of Shiva, one Brahman came to her and stated:

> I am a disciple of Shiva and he is my Guru. It is true that he besmears his body with dust, wears skin of leapods, elephants and other animals, and wraps snakes around his neck and body. He eats poison and looks from three eyes. As such, his appearance is dreadful. He lives in the company of goblins and evil spirits. You are a princess and he is not fit to be your husband, for he is a poor beggar. Your father is the king of the mountains and owns much wealth, treasure and palaces. Why should you marry a mendicant? You are beautiful and he is ugly. You are rich and he is poor. He cannot keep you happy.

Hearing all this, Parvati admonished the Brahman. She told him that none can separate her from her lover and she would ultimately win her love: "I am for Shiva and he is for me"! When Manika heard that her daughter loved a mendicant named Shiva, she became very sad. She decided that she will not give her daughter in marriage to Shiva. The king decided to convene the Suyambara of her daughter and invited all princes of the land. All palaces and gardens of the capital were decorated with illumination. The road to the main palace was decorated with bunting and flowers. For guests, many luxurious palaces were built by the king, who invited all the kings of the Himalayas to witness the marriage of his daughter.

Shiva invited all the gods to participate in this function.

1. Shiva-Maha-Purana; Sati Khand, p. III

Shiva was decorated in a beautiful attire and ornaments. Brahma became the manager of the marriage procession, which included Brahma, Vishnu and Indra. The front row consisted of musicians, who were playing *dumroo* and *shank*. Shiva wore the moon on his head and looked like a very beautiful groom. He looked extremely handsome when he rode on his bull. When the marriage party reached near the palace, every one lined himself or herself to receive the groom. In the meanwhile, thoughts of suspicion arose in the heart of Manika, with the result that Shiva understood her mind. He at once changed his appearance and exhibited himself as a mendicant. He looked as a naked beggar in the company of beggars and goblins. All those accompanying him looked as vagabonds and ruffians. Shiva wore a garland of skulls and looked hedious. Seeing this the queen suffered a shock and cried that she would never give her daughter in marriage to a beggar.[1]

Hearing this, Shiva started his Thandava dance. As the rhythm went on, snow started falling. Then it changed into silver and gold. There occurred a rain of diamonds and all marvelled. The king and the queen repented and agreed to give Parvati in marriage to Shiva. Every body worshipped him and there were slogans of joy from all sides. Thus after this heavenly marriage, Shiva and Parvati retired to the sacred cave of eternal bliss.

Shivratri or the marriage night of Shiva is being observed in Kashmir as one of the greatest festivals. It is always accompanied with a snow-fall. According to the Nila-mata-purana, the valley of Kashmir is the manifestation of Shiva and Shakti. Among the most important shrines of Kashmir, the Amarnatha cave is foremost and as such, the abode of Shiva.

Parvati, as the supreme Mother is worshipped by all. She is the mother of the universe and the supreme power. She is Maha Sakhti, Kundalini, Durga, Devi and Mahakali.

---

1. Shiva-Maha-Purana. Sati-Khand.

O Divine Mother! You are the Queen of Heaven!
All Devas, Devis, gods and goddesses,
All saints, men and women,
Adore and worship Thee,
Thy feet are adored even by Brahma, Vishnu and Rudra.

Sri Amarnatha Cave

The holy cave of Sri Amarnatha is nested among bare mountains at a height of 12,729 ft. above the sea level. It is 17 meters long and 14 meters wide. Its roof is about 14 meters high. The cave can hold hundreds of visitors at a time and there is no danger of suffocation due to wide entrance.

In the South-eastern corner of the holy cave, the pilgrims see the self-formed ice Lingam, in a reclining position. The water drops from the ceiling of the cave fall on the base and get frozen, with the result that some erected icicles are formed due to freezing of successive drops. The huge icicle is the immortal Lingam of Shiva, while the small icicles are the emblems of his consort or son. The main Lingam is believed to wax and wane according to the phases of moon.

The above is the physical description of the Lingam of Shiva, but for the devotees, it is the darshan of God.

Route from Pahalgam

The route from Pahalgam to the holy cave of Sri Amarnatha, covers the following stages:

Pahalgam
Chandanwari
Waojan
Panjtarni
Amarnatha

All the pilgrims assemble at Pahalgam on the 11th of Sawan, which falls in July-August every year. Next morning, the procession starts for Chandanwari, which is 16 kms. from Pahalgam. On their way, some of the devotees take bath in the Nila-ganga stream, while others go straightaway to

Chandanwari. It is better to reach the destination as early as possible, so that a tent could be got fixed at a better site. From Chandanwari to the Pissu hill is a difficult ascent. One must make an early start and cross the snow bed. Before proceeding to Sheshram-nag, it is advisible to eat something. The spring of Sheshram-nag lies by the glacier on the flank of the Pissu hill. From this place the next stage of the journey ends at Waojan. It is a camping site situated at the height of 12,230 ft. above the sea level.

From Waojan, the pilgrims proceed to Panjtarni. In the way they pass through Mahagunas, which is a big plateau. After passing Hoksar, Kalinar, the pilgrims reach a huge boulder, known as Nagarapal. Every pilgrim has to throw two pebbles on this boulder, so as to beat the demon. After walking further, one reaches the Panjtarni stream. Now the pilgrims have to take bath and purify themselves, before reaching the holy cave. Every visitor has to pitch his tent here at the site for the night.

From Panjtarni, one has to go only 7 kms. to reach the sacred cave of Amarnatha. After passing over a small glacier, one reaches a large cave-like hole in the mountain. Inside this cave is the abode of Shiva, known as Sri Amarnatha.

Route via Sonamarg

Those visitors, who avoid the traditional route of Pahalgam, reach the sacred cave of Amarnatha, *via* Sonamarg. This new route takes less time and is safe. This route is as under:

Sonamarg
Baltal
Sangam
Amarnatha cave

From Sonamarg, the pilgrims start for Baltal by vehicles and reach that place in an hour. From that place, some prefer to go on horse-back, while many prefer trekking. After a distance of about 3 kms. a very steep ascent starts. The route is dangerous at certain points and one should proceed carefully. After a walk of a few miles, the pilgrims and visitors reach Sangam. The holy cave is only 5 kms. away from this stage. After some distance, one has to cross over an avalanche of glacier. The sacred cave is near at hand surrounded by mighty mountains.

Worship of the Lingam

From ancient time, the devotees from far off regions of the country have been visiting the sacred cave of Sri Amarnatha, to have the darshan of Shiva-Lingam. For them every particle of earth, sand and rock, every drop of water and every leaf of vegetation is sacred at this site. They first wash themselves and then apply *Amar-vibhuti*, or the chalky clay on their foreheads. Wearing white cloths or naked, they enter the cave, so as to become one with the Supreme.

The pilgrims offer camphor, candy, pepper and candles to the deity. Some offer silver, gold and currency. The Vedas and Tantras are recited, before the two snow pigeons fly out of the cave. It is a good omen and the pilgrims clap their hands and shout in ecstasy.

O Mother of the world, O Mother!
I have not worshipped Thy feet,
Nor have I given abundant wealth to Thee,
Yet the affection which Thou bestowest on me is without compare
For, a bad son may sometimes be born, but a bad mother never.

Amareshvara Mahatmya

Shiva Amareshvara manifested himself to the gods, in the cave of Amarnatha. Since ancient times, this sacred abode of the Lord has been the most important Tirtha of the devotees, in the valley of Kashmir. The *Amareshvara Mahatmya* describes the route leading to the immortal self-created ice Lingam, in question and answer form. Parvati, the Divine consort asks questions, which are answered by the Lord himself. It starts as under:

O Deva! O Parma—Shiva!
Thee are the Brahman!

Thee are the Atamn!
Thee are the Guru!
Salutations to Thee!

O Blessed Bhairava! O Parmeshvara!
O Deva! O Shiva! I have heard often of the sacredness of Martand and Anantnag. I wish to listen now to the importance of the pilgrimage to Amareshvara. I understand that after listening to the nectar story of Shiva-Lingam in the sacred cave, one attains liberation. O Lord of Lords and Ocean of Mercy! Please tell me here and now what would be the fate of those pilgrims, who visit the Tirtha, without having visited the shrines *en route* to Sri Amareshvara.

The Lord felt much pleased to hear the above from the lips of his consort. They had just visited the sun temple of Martand, which is situated on the plateau of Matan. It is one of the most celebrated shrines in the valley. At the foot of the western extremity of Martand plateau lies the sacred spring of Anantnag. Bhairava looked lovingly towards his beloved and said:

Salutations to you, my Bhairavi! You are Uma,
Gauri, Durga and Sharada!
You are beautiful like a chain of lightning.
You are fine like a lotus flower.
O Divine Spouse! You are the Life of all lives.

O Devi! Please listen! I shall now relate all about the pilgrimage to the holy Cave. One who even hears with devotion the story of the pilgrimage, shall be put at par with the one, who had actually visited the shrine. A visit without full knowledge of the greatness of Lord Shiva would be as futile as incurring the sin of betraying the holy pilgrimage.

O Dear! The pilgrimage should begin with holy dips in Shodash-hetar (Shurayar), Shiv Pora, Pad-dwashti (Pandrethan) and a sip of water at Padampur (Pampore), with another dip in Sidhkhetar (Sidyar). O Maheshwari!

Taking dips in Ruder-ganga (Warish) and Yuti (Jaw Broor) Mishthod (Methwani), Awantika (Awantipora) and Sidh-khetar (Pahalgam), obtains great merits for the devotees.

The Lord here speaks about ablutions to be performed at sacred ponds and springs. Shurayar is at the foot of the Sankracharya hill, where existed the pond of Shodash Khetar. From this place a stone staircase leads to the Temple of Solomon. Before starting for the pilgrimage of Shri Amareshvara, it is essential to have a dip in the pond of Shurayar. Unfortunately, the pond does not exist now. Pandrethan was the old capital of the kingdom of Kashmir. There exists the famous miniature temple in the middle of a spring. Mishthod means sweet water and the spring was famous for its freshness.

O Sundri! with a sip of water of Maha-naga (Mehar-nag) having taken a dip in Jaishtshada, proceed to the village Haridra and worship god Ganpati. After this, take a dip in the Vidhman-kund and Balihar. Having arrived at Uagh-Ashram, worship Harti-Karam, the Shrine of Ganpati and take a sip of water. Continue to take dips in Chakreshwari and Devki-tirath, for it contains many merits.

Kashmir, to its Shiavites is pre-eminently the land of Shiva and Shakti or Bhairava and Bhairavi. The number of such Bhairava and Bhairavi tirthas is a legion. All the *nags* or springs in the valley are divine and sacred. The water of these springs is nectar of life. By taking a bath in some, you are purified both physically and spiritually. The Lord addresses his consort as follows:

O Bhairavi! O Goddess! Salutations to Thee.
O Dear! With a dip in Harichandar (Chandanyar), O Maheshwari, with a dip in the sacred spring of Sathol-watt, worship the sun god and proceed to the place Ghuwatt. There with full devotion take a dip in the river Lambodari (Lidar).[1] Having arrived in Surya-

1. This river, ancient Ledari receives a number of streams, during its course towards Khanbal, where it joins the river Vitasta.

Ashram (Sirhama), take a dip in sacred Surya-Ganga and make offerings and gifts, whereby the sin of having killed any living being would be wiped off.

In Kashmir, Shiva's female consort is described as having somewhat superior position than that of Shiva. Kashmir is in itself Bhairavi and as such, manifestation of herself. The Lord also, here addresses his divine consort as Maheshvari.

Ghuwatt or Gohawati is a village between Thajwor and Sirhom and is now known as Sirigpure. This Tiratha is sacred to Ganpati whose worship removes all obstacles in life.

Mammeshvara

The Lord gives the description of the sacred Tirtha of Mammeshvara as under:

O Bhairavi! Salutations to Thee!
O Uma! O Sati! O Gauri! I bow to Thee!

O Great Goddess! Then onwards, taking bath in a place named Sakharas worshipping Ganesha who removes obstacles, one should proceed to Badhoras. O Goddess! After taking dips in the Utternag situated in Havshrisashram and in the Ganges situated in Badhoras, one should go to the village Sarlak. O Dear! After taking a dip there one should worship great god Vishnu in the village Khilvavan. Again after taking another dip in the oldest holy place, Naravana, one should proceed ahead to the holy village named Mamlak and worship Ganesh. After worshipping the holy Lingam at Mammeshvara and taking dips in the holy water of Mammesh-Kund and Nilganga, situated in Bragupati (Pahalgam); crossing the holy river in Sathanwa-Ashram (Chandanwari); which washes away the sins of many numerous births, then proceed to the Peshgiri hill (Pishbal), which destroys all sins. After taking dips in Seshrumnag and Yavnwargam (Yawagam), one attains great divine merits. In this holy place, as an act of piety pilgrims may erect small beautiful cottages.

Shiva being fond of his consort, addresses her as great goddess.

He also explains the advantages of taking dips in holy water.

The most sacred temple of Mammeshwara Lingam exists at Mamal in Pahalgam. King Jayasimha (1128-49 A.D.) is reported to have furnished the shrine with a golden parasol.[1] The Tirtha at Mamal came into prominence when Shiva changed his seat from Thojwat to this site, situated on the hill-side opposite the Pahalgam market. The Mammeshwara Lingam should be worshipped before the pilgrims proceeds to Sri Amar Nath.

The Mammeshwara Lingam is the real Lingam of Shiva. In fact everything is Shiva's Lingam, in the inner and the outer world. It may be emphasised that Shiva is himself his own Lingam. In fact the Lingam is only a symbol of Shiva in the act of creation. It is the truth made concrete which depicts the divine origin of humanity.

Shiva continued his discourse as under:

> Following what with a dip in the sacred river of Panchtarni ascend the mount, and then go between Garbh Yatra after a dip in the holy river of Amravati apply *vibhuti* on the bare body, chanting the name and hymns of Lord Shiva, enter the cave of Amareshvara. Complying with the edicts of Vedas and Shastras, adhering to the rituals with due devotion, one gets rid of all the sins of past births. By seeing and touching the Shiva Lingam, uttering mantra offering flowers, one again gets free of all sorts of sins.

Shiva the Lord of creation gets very pleased with hymns sung in his praise. One who chants the hymns in devotion to Bhairava is absolved of all sins. The touch of the Shiva Lingam at Amareshvara cave gets much wealth, long life, many children as also fame in this world. After his death, such a devotee goes to the abode of Shiva and remains there in great glory.

O Great Goddess! O Granter of Siddhis!

---

1. Rajatarngini; Kalhana, trans, Stein, viii, 3360.

> O Bhairavi! Proceed then to the holy place named Mamlak and worship Ganpati with full devotion. While worshipping Ganpati, one has to use varieties of tilak, *dhup*, sweets, *purees* and flowers. After worshipping Ganesh with all these offerings, one should go to the bank of Ganga in the village Navdal and should offer a stick to a learned Brahman. O Great Mother! the instructions for taking six dips in the holy Vitasta and seventeen dips in the *Kunds* at different places has been quoted in Smriti. One has to visit twenty-three holy places in the sacred Amarnatha Yatra. Thus, completing the whole pilgrimage, human beings can get the pleasure of the holy darshan of Raslingam and attain such high spiritual attainments that there is no feeling of sin or virtues. In conclusion, the darshan of Amareshvara Lingam, in the holy cave achieves eternal peace and is glorified in the abode of sinner being freed from all sins.

After the darshan, the devotees find peace and bliss. They feel one with Shiva, the creator, the protector and the destroyer of the world. There is no god better than Shiva, there is no better hymn than the hymn in praise of Shiva, and there is no lovely word than the name of Shiva Shakti. The delightful conversation between Shiva and his consort continues as follows:

> O Lord, thy greatness is beyond the reach of mind and speech. O Lord, I want to hear about the Khilyan. Kindly relate to me as to what happened in the holy village of Khilyan while erecting the holy place as the Tirtha of Narayana.[1] Narayana is Vishnu, the Giver of *vibhuti*. The whole creation is the *vibhuti* of Vishnu.

When Bhairavi asked this question, the Lord has already destroyed the three cities and the demons at the prayer of the gods. Well, Shiva was but playing with things, when he replied:

---

1. Khilyan is known as Bala Khilyan now. During old times, it was known as Vishnu-Khetra or the village of Vishnu.

O Devi! Great Goddess! Listen, I am going to describe the holy place Khilyan, after listening which the human beings get rid of all sins. O Beloved of Shiva! In ancient times, many great saints were practising rigid penance in the village of Khilyan, who were known as Balkhil Yogis. Having conquered and subdued their senses, they were living without food and water for thousands of years. They were standing on their toes absorbed in *Samadhi*. With that peace of mind they were meditating on Lord Vishnu.

Vishnu-Khetra

Before the advent of Shaivaism in Kashmir, Vishnuism occupied an important place among the people. Vishnu is a solar deity, praised by Brahma and Shiva. He is always available in rescue operations, such as grant of boons and destruction of demons. He is four-armed, four-faced, having complexion like snow, lotus-eyed, wearing a crown of jewels. His mount is Garuda and he lies on the jewelled hood of the king snake, with his consort, Lakshmi. Lord Vishnu is the preserver of the world. Krishna is the incarnation of Vishnu. The whole creation is the *vibhuti* of Lord Vishnu.

Shiva, the Lord of the gods, continued his discourse as under:

At last, Lord Vishnu appeared before the meditating monks. His mount was Garuda, the enemy of the Nagas. His weapons included sword, club, disc and bow and he held lotus and conch in his hands. Seeing the Lord, the saints prostrated before him and chanted mantaras in his praise.

The saints continue their prayers and praises:

O Lord! You are great, you are all powerful, you are worthy of worshipping full of resplendent; you carry the burden of the whole universe; you are unique and we surrender at your lotus feet. You are incarnation of Vedas; you are the wisdom of Vedas; you are the most primal and all purifying. You are *Hirmija-garba*. You are the foremost

Lord of all gods. You are the mighty long armed and we take shelter under your lotus feet. You are Lord of the three worlds and our protector.

The saints continue recitation of hymns as under:

O, Lord You are the source of the universe. You are worthy of receiving offerings from three worlds. You are the greatest. You are the Lord of the universe. You are all providing. You are the oldest and the soul of the universe; we take refuge at your sacred feet. O Lord! you are the great actor whereby through your power of illusion, within moments, you take the appearance of a baby; an youth as well as a man and woman. We all surrender at your effulgent divine appearance.

O Bhairavi! Thou are the giver of everlasting bliss. O Dear! After offering prayers to Lord Vishnu, they fell down on his holy feet, and the Lord got them up. The Lord started delivering his sermon which was similar to the roaring of clouds: "I am pleased with your rigid penance and devotion. You can now ask for any boon from me. Though that boon may not be available to gods and demons, but I must give it to you." After hearing such powerful speech from the Lord, the Balkhil yogis begged of him as under:

"O God, what can be more greater boon to us than your holy appearance. Then also being asked by you for boon, we pray for a supreme holy place from you, such as the sight of that holy place can obtain sacred thought and salvation. O Narayana! Let there be the most sacred Tirtha of yours for all of us. Let it rise high up to the heavens."

When Vishnu heard all this, he became very pleased with the saints. They had taken refuge in him and he became very kind to them.

After hearing these holy words, the Lord looked at his holy feet with the tears of joy and made the Ganges to flow. Along with this, in order to glorify the Ashrams of those saints who had the complete knowledge of *Atam*, the village of the Lord is known Khilyan. This place is most sacred and removes all sorts of obstacles. This place shall become an important pilgrimage, known as Vishnu-Khetra. Soon after delivering the sermon Lord Vishnu vanished. By reason of having performed penance by these great successful saints and by the reason of appearance of Lord Vishnu personally, the village became most important and hence it is named as Bala Khilyan or Vishnu-Khetra.

Since this place has become purified and has the setting of the feet of Lord Narayana, it is renowned as Narayan Tirtha also. If any human being takes a dip in this Narayan Tirtha, all of his simple and worst sins shall be washed away at once. Those who are afraid of the impacts of Kalyuga should without any hesitation take bath in this Narayan Tirtha. The sins of having taken intoxicating drinks shall be washed out by taking a sip of water of this Narayan Tirtha.

After saying all the above, Shiva thus addressed his consort:

> O dear, there is no doubt at all that a sip of water of this Tirtha shall purify the sins of a person, who had taken the prohibited food and drinks. Any man or woman who takes bath in this Tirtha, will certainly attain liberation.

The Lord further said that the water of this Tirtha was just like the nectar of life and sure to give inner bliss. Shiva has great affection and regard for Vishnu, for he is always pleased with his devotion. The story goes that Vishnu would worship the Lord, daily with one thousand lotuses. One day, Shiva, in order to test the devotion of Vishnu, stole away one lotus out of one thousand lotuses. At the time of prayers, when Vishnu could not find the one lotus, he plucked his one eye and offered it as one lotus. On seeing such devotion, Shiva, felt very much pleased with Vishnu and gave him powers to protect the three worlds.

Shiva continues his talk with Bhairavi as under:

> O Bhairavi! You are the embodiment of all bliss.
> You are the awakener of pure knowledge.
> O Bhairavi! My salutations to Thee! O Devi!

O Sundari! Every sinner must do five things to wash off his sins. He must utter mantaras, offer Homa, do Japa, visit Tirthas and feed the Brahmanas.

After telling the above, the Lord deals with other sinners and tells as to how they can obtain liberation.

O Parvati! Thee embodiment of grace!
O Dear! One responsible for abortion; killer of a Brahman; false Sanyasi; husband of a low caste woman; killer of cows; one who goes to his wife during menstrual period and developing a lust of it; one who poisons some body; burns some body; an armed looter; killer of a lady or child, will also attain liberation within six months, by observing penance at this Tirtha.

Shiva gives a detailed description of merits, which can be obtained from pilgrimage of the Tirtha of Narayana.

O Devi! You are resplendent like the lusters of many suns. Please listen with attention. After taking a dip in the holiest place of Lord Vishnu situated in Khilyan village, one gets rid of all his sins which he has committed throughout his life beyond any doubt. O blessed! If one does not make any effort to get his sins washed off but dies in the holy place of Lord Vishnu, situated in the Khilyan village, he obtains darshan of the lotus feet of Lord Vishnu and thus gets liberation from all his anxieties. Either taking a bath in this most holy place of Lord Vishnu, according to the injunction of scriptures or taking a sip of water, one gets rid of all sins which he has committed in his past numerous births; because there was no such pilgrimage like Khilyan in the past nor will it be in the future.

Shiva further relates the merits of visiting the Tirtha of Vishnu in the following words:

O Devi! Thy glories be praised. O Bhairavi!
O Devi! It is really difficult to be fortunate enough to make offerings at village Khilyan. Hence one should adhere to

strict meditation at that place. O Devi! Taking dips to ones satisfaction or taking a sip of water at this holy place result in increasing one's life span, earning fame and virtues and destruction of all terrible sins.

The Lord continues to praise Vishnu-Khetra in the following words:

> O Bhairavi! O Sundari! O Parvati!
> Narayana is situated in Khilyan that there is no doubt in the fact that one gets salvation after visiting the holy place. A person gets liberation by taking a bath, making donation, doing penance and worshipping in the holy place of Lord Vishnu, situated in the sacred village of Khilyan. It is a matter of a great mystery that this pilgrimage of Lord Vishnu is full of innumerable virtues.

It was in this way that Bhairava described the Tirtha of Vishnu to his divine consort. While offering three handful of flowers and three libations of the consecrated drink to her, the Lord said:

> O goddess!
> May you be kind to me.
> May you accept my prayer and praise.
> May you visit the sacred Tirtha of Narayana.
> O Beloved!
> Accept my salutations again and again.
> Glory be to you.
> For you have occupied half of my body:
> Through devotion, love and affection.

It was in these words that the Lord of the universe praised the daughter of the mountains.

CHAPTER II

Amareshvara Cave

Salutations to Lord Shiva,
Who is Omnipresent, Omnipotent and Omniscient,
Who is above the triple qualities of,
Satawa, Rajas and Tamas.

Bhairava is united with his spouse, Bhairavi, and together they visit the Tirthas of Kashmir. During one such retreat the Goddess tells her Lord:

O Lord, Rudra, Sarva, Bhava and Mahadeva! Thou are my beloved and I bow down. O lover of solitude, my salutations to thee, who are very near!
O Parmeshvara! You are the creator, the protector, and the destroyer of the worlds.
You are known to all as Parama-Shiva!
In you is united both *Rasa* and *Virasa*.

The Lord of the three worlds addresses his divine consort as follows:

O Bhagavati! You are as lustrous as the light of all the suns shining at one and the same time. You are the mother of the three worlds.
You contain within you the stream of excellent nectar.

Bhairavi asked this question:

O God! may I ask a question? O Lord!
Thou are indeed pleasing and thrill me with joy. After

listening to the importance of sacred pilgrimage of Narayana at village Khilyan from your sacred mouth, I have also attained supreme bliss. Now I want to listen to the beautiful story of pilgrimage to Mamal which destroys even the worst sins.

When Bhairava waited for a moment, the divine consort again said:

O Lord! Your Tirtha at Mamal contains a large number of perfect Lingams.
The main Lingam has been covered with a golden Amalaka.
O Lord! I am so dear to you and your kind blessings are bestowed upon me; kindly tell me how Lord Ganpati was established in the Tirtha of Mammeshvara?

Bhairava being in a very happy mood, was ready to grant any boon to the humanity. He said as under:

Bhairavi! listen I am going to tell you about the sacred pilgrimage of Mammeshvara, simply by visiting which one overcomes obstacles. In ancient time this place of destroying sins was named after a devotee. I was pleased with his rigid penance and devotion for me. I arranged his stay at Sathoolwat where one gets rid of all obstacles of life easily.
In fact, you are that unspeakable truth, which Yogis realize through meditation.
O Devi! Indeed you are that unspeakable truth, realizing which, they swim, as it were, in a pool of nectar.

Hearing this from the sweet lips of Bhairava, Parvati felt elated and pleased. She said:

O Lord ! Please do not shower praises on me. I know what I am ! Please proceed further about the pilgrimage to Mammeshvara.

The Lord continued as under:

After going ahead from Khilyan through the forest of Dhandak Muni, he sat there for a while and in the meantime all the gods also collected there with pleasing attitude. On seeing gods, this devotee cried loudly: 'O gods ! do not come here! Ganpati appeared hurriedly from underworld with an axe in his hand, addressing the gods:

Please do not come here!

The gods felt amazed to hear the sweet voice of Ganpati. Because getting absorbed in eternal peace with Brahma, Creator of the universe, this place came to be known as Mamal.

O Dear! seeing Ganpati come from underworld, Lord Shiva addressed Ganpati in these words: "you should stay here at Mammeshvara for ever to remove the obstacles coming in the way of all my devotees". Whosoever worships Ganpati here will win over all the obstacles and will succeed in getting liberation. One who prays Ganpati here will get all his ambitions fulfilled and even obtain children, wealth and liberation.

Having uttered these sacred words, Shiva engulfed in the heavenly embrace of his spouse and said:

O Beautiful One!
Thou are the Sun!
Thou are the Moon!
Thou are the Fire!
Thou are the Air!
Thou are the Water!
Thou are the Space!

He had uttered only these praises, when Bhairavi placed her fingers on the lips of her Lord, saying:

O Lord! All praise is due to Thee.
Thou are the Self!
To Thee, who are beloved
I bow down.
O Beloved! May you please continue?

Shiva thus spoke further to Parvati:

O Devi! My salutation to Thee. I tell you the truth. Whosoever visits this place on 14th day of moonlit night in the month of *Vaishakh* and meditates throughout the night, keeping himself on fast, will have all the ambitions, in this world, fulfilled and will attain the abode of Lord Shiva after his death.

Bhairavi had heard all the above with attention. She was calm and serene and wished to her more from the sweet lips of her Lord. Shiva continued as under:

O Parameshvari! This universe is illuminated by your radiance.

O Sundari! You are the awakener of eternal knowledge. Please Listen! The person who prays Ganpati at Mammeshvara on the night mentioned above, will attain eternal bliss. O Devi! Any one who worships you at Mammeshvara will achieves great virtues. In this way, Lord Shiva after blessing Ganpati himself fell in Samadhi in sacred Dandak forest and this place came to be known as Mammeshvara. A person after sighting the Lingam of Mammeshvara at the sacred village of Mamlak and by saluting Lord Ganpati there, gets the fruits similar to the performance of *Ashma-Meg-Yaga.*

Any one who wants to attain merit must worship the pure Lingam. Its darshan, results in health, wealth and long life. The gods have worshipped the Lingam and attained merit. Shiva Lingam is the cause and result of the world. Once it happened that it fell down from the hands of Shiva. When it fell on the earth, the surface began to burn, it rose towards the sky; there also is caused fire. Brahma knew that it is the manifestation of Shiva and as such, collected gods to tell them all about it. The Lingam would cause the destruction of all the planets and there could be no peace until the Lingam would rest in the Yoni. After many prayers, Parvati agreed to receive the Lingam. She changed herself into Yoni. When prayers were going on, the Lingam came and settled in the Yoni. Peace prevailed and the world was saved from destruction.

Hence the gods have said that anyone who wants to save himself from destruction must worship the Shiva Lingam daily. The Lingam at Mammeshvara Tirtha is the real Lingam of Bhairava. Its greatness is accepted by the gods and praises of even gods are inadequate for it.

Bhairavi requested Shiva to continue telling her the merits to be obtained from a pilgrimage of the Tirtha of Mammeshvara. Bhairava says as under:

O Devi! You constitute a part of the Lingam.
Indeed you yourself are the Lingam.
Both Bhairavi and Bhairava are united at Mammeshvara.
O Parvati! After seeing Ganpati near Mammeshvara and after praying him according to the scriptures, one is blessed with ever-lasting success.

O Bhairavi! You are Devi Lingam.
O Bhairavi! You are Shakti Lingam.
O Bhairavi! You are Shiva Lingam.

It is to be noted that together with Shiva, the Devi is the cause of all the Lingams in this material as well as in the spiritual world. In fact, Bhairavi is herself the Lingam by nature.

After having described the merits, one can atttain by having a dip in the spring of Mammeshvara, Bhairava speaks as follows:

O Bhairavi! You are the seed.
O Bhairavi! You are the receptacle.
O Bhairavi! You are the cause.

O Father of the universe!
O Mother of the world! One who worships Ganpati in the sacred village of Mamal will never be effected by great obstacles; evil stars can neither harm him in this world nor in the other world. Those who worship naturally born Ganpati at Mammeshvara attain the fruits of *Joti Ashitam Yaga*. After seeing the god Ganpati at Mamal, a person

with Vedic rituals, who has conquered his senses attains the fruits of *Soma Yaga.*

The Lord continued the discourse as under:

O Devi! god Ganpati is *Vigan-raja* and selfish persons can free themselves from selfish nature by having seen *Vigan-raja.* It must be known that the glimpse of the god, vanishes all grave sins. O goddess! A pilgrimage to *Vigan-raja* would save a devotee from all obstacles.

O Beloved! I have told you all about the sacred cave of Sri Amareshwara. I hope you are pleased to hear all what I said.

The divine consort felt pleased and expressed herself as follows:

O Lord of the Universe!

O Lord of gods, can the worlds be without its creator? My salutation to you, O Great God. I have achieved great pleasure to hear about the sacred story of *Vigan-raja* from your sweet lips. If I am your beloved and blessed, then relate to me, the significance of the sacred Lambodhari?

The Three-eyed one continued as under:

O Bhairavi! you are the Creator, the Preserver and the Soul. You are the Moon, the Sun, the Sky and the Air. In fact you are Shiva and Shakti.

O Bhairavi! These are the different names by which you are heard of and called by the devotees.

O Bhairavi! Let the gods relate the story of our previous life as under:

Ganpati

It so happened that Parvati was having a bath along with her friends when Shiva entered the premises without intimation. Goddess Parvati and her friends felt embarrassed. An idea occurred to her that she must have an obedient door-keeper, who should be posted at the door. Ganpati was born out of this wish. One day the goddess ordered him not to allow anyone enter into her palace without first seeking permission. Ganpati heard and assured that he shall carry out her orders faithfully. At that very moment, Shiva came and tried to enter the door but was stopped by Ganpati. The Lord told Ganpati that Parvati was his consort and as such, he had every right to enter the premises. But Ganpati refused to oblige him saying that he was doing his duty and would not allow anyone to enter without the permission of Parvati.[1]

"One day Lord Shiva was having a rest at Kailash mountain and Ganpati was deputed as watchman. The very moment Lord Shiva told Ganpati that no one should trespass the premises. "You should make even gods halt". Listening to the instructions of Lord Shiva, Ganpati along with Nandi checked every one in obedience of Lord Shiva. Then Lord Shiva began to converse with Parvati. Thereafter, both Shiva and Parvati began to live gracefully on the Kailash mountain.

May Parvati, the wife of the Lord.
Ward off harm.
She in whose half,
The adorable one,
Took up his residence,
After leaving outside.[2]

"In the meantime, teased by Tripura Sur, god Indra Deva along with other gods came to see Lord Shiva. Ganpati stopped them from entering the premises. At this, Indra furiously enraged, took his weapon in his hand. Ganpati also in furry, struck his weapon on his arm. On seeing the deep injury on his arm, Indra saluted god Ganpati and worshipped him in melodious voice."

1. Shiva-purana; 4 : I3
2. Rajatarangini; 8 : 1

O god Ganpati! Our salutations to you.
O god Ganpati! O Remover of obstacles.

Thou are full of numerous virtues, worshipped by gods, revered by the sages.
You are almighty in the shape of Omkar.
O Son of the Lord! You are equal to Shiva,
O Beloved son of Parvati! Our salutations to you.
We bow to you who is almighty, eternal, glorious, endless and the beginning of all pacred chants.
O god Ganpati! Our salutations to thee.
O Ganpati! All the gods bow to you.
O Ganpati! full of virtues and grace, we salute thee repeatedly.

In this way, Shiva removed the doubts of his divine consort. She continues to make quiry and requests the Lord to complete the story of the Lidari. Bhairava accedes to her request and says:

In this way, after hearing the sacred prayers of Indra, god Ganpati's anger came to an end, and he began to look upon Indra mercifully. He with immense pleasure freed Indra's arm from the arm which he had struck earlier.

Bhairava continues his discourse and tells about the etymology of the river the Lidari, in the following words:

After saluting Ganpati, Indra full of satisfied desires, left for his home. Thereafter any person, who sincerely recites hymns of god Ganpati; the vanisher of all worries and anxieties, three times a day, morning, noon and evening, will get rid of all sins and obstacles. O Devi ! thereafter, the hungry and thirsty Ganesh, after taking the sweet fruits, swallowed the whole water of Ganges. As he had drunk all the water of this river, his belly swelled.

It was after this incident that the Lord named Ganpati as Lambodhar.

Shiva continues the story of Ganpati as under:

O Dear ! After seeing dry Ganges, I struck the belly of Ganpati with my *damroo* and by which, Ganges came out from the mouth of the god. It is that water of the Ganges which flowed from the mouth of god Ganpati and is called by ancient learned men as the Lidari river. After taking a dip in this holy river, a person gets rid of all his numerous births.

O Great Goddess! All grave sins are destroyed even by touching the sacred waters of the river Lidari.

Those who bath in the waters of the pious Lidari with great devotion and with right rituals, are freed from all dark and grave sins. O Devi! He who bath in the sacred Lidari with immense pleasure and devotion, attain great virtues and is not teased by any wordly sufferings. Such are the merits one achieves by taking a bath in the sacred river.

On a further enquiry by the divine consort, Bhairava said as under:

O Bhairavi! To thee who are beloved and effulgent, I bow. O Dear! Sinners must wash out their sins and that is only possible if they dip in the holy waters of the Lidari. O Devi! Every sinner must dip in these holy waters, for it gushes out of the mouth of your dear son, god Ganpati.

O Bhairavi! Let every devotee of yours obtain bliss by hearing the description of the Lidari. O Devi! Let the sinners of the world hear that their dark and horrible sins would be washed, if they abide by the instructions.

Bragu Tirtha

Shiva and Parvati flew over the high mountains and selected a beautiful spot for retreat. Many centuries passed away and the gods could not find their resort. One day, Shiva being in a jolly mood, and in order to tease Parvati, told her, "O Devi! You have a black complexion!"

Hearing such a remark from her lover, the divine consort in a resenting mood said: "O God! I am black, then why did you consider me as your beloved for all these centuries! Under such circumstances, it is better for me to make an end of my present life." After having said the above, Parvati desired to leave. Feeling that his words had created a row, Shiva said:

O Bhairavi! You are dear to me than life. I had uttered some words in a joking way and you felt that I was talking seriously. You have become angry with me.

O Dearest! You are the Mother of Universe and I am the Father of Creation. You are in me and I am in you. You are my love and I am your love. Did not I destroy Kama because our love is divine.

After a moment, Parvati requested her Lord to tell her something about Bragu Tirtha. Bhairava said:

O Devi! My salutation to you. I will gladly reply your question. O Goddess! Listen, now I will describe the ancient and wonderful story of Bragu Tirtha. O Goddess! In ancient times, a great and a successful saint named Bragu, who was much devoted, performed a rigid penance. He passed one thousand years during his penance and achieved *Maha Samadhi*. After seeing great and unselfish devotion of the saint Bragu, Lord Vishnu along with all gods, appeared with illuminating appearance before this devotee. Having darshan of the Lord, the saint worshipped Lord Vishnu with his sweet and attractive words. His hymn is as follows:

O Almighty! Have mercy, have mercy,
Who is the God to whom we shall offer our salutation?
He who gives life.

O Almighty Lord Vishnu! Thou are worshipped and praised by gods. Thou are omnipresent, full of gracious virtues. Thou are eternal and merciful. I bow my head at your lotus feet.

Affter praising Lord Vishnu, saint Bragu fell on the lotus feet of his Lord repeatedly. Seeing pure devotion of his disciple, Lord Vishnu, who is eternal and the shelter of this Universe, was pleased with penance of saint Bragu. The Lord embraced his devotee with tears of love in his eyes.

When Bragu and Lord Vishnu embraced each other, pure love was illuminated all around. O Goddess! then after sweat came out from their bodies and the drops of water are sign and proof of pure devotion; became a holy pilgrimage in Parishool forest. O great Goddess! It is the basic and holy story of Bragu Tirtha famed since ancient times. At Bragu Tirtha, with a dip of water and a sip of water and by offering gifts, even those who are killers of human beings achieve good virtues and divine bliss.

> O Devi! The above are the merits, one attains by visiting Bragu Tirtha. By offering gifts, at the Tirtha, one gets satisfaction, solace and bliss.
> O Bhairavi! Even the great sinners of Kalyuga will be freed from their grave sins, at the time they arrive at the Tirtha.

Bhairava was very pleased with Bhairavi. He addressed her in a loving mood:

> O Beautiful! the whole world bows to have your sight. You are the Light.
> O Lustrous one! With fortune you shine on all the gods.
> O Gracious one! You are kind, generous and merciful.

Bhairavi feeling pleased with the praises of the Lord said:

> O God! There is no god better than you.
> O Bhairava! There is no hymn better than the hymn in praise of you.
> O Beloved! If the ocean be ink, the branches of all heavenly trees be pen, the earth be the writing pad, and if Sarvasti writes for eternity, even then the limits of your virtues will not be touched.

Nila Ganga

Bhairavi had the story of Bragu Tirtha from the mouth of the Lord. Now she wished to hear about the Nila Ganga:

> O Beautiful! I obtained great pleasure on hearing the holy story and excellencies of Bragu Tirtha at Parshool forest, which is the destroyer of all sins and evils of the universe. Now, I wish to listen to the evolution of Nila Ganga, which eradicates the clusters of sins of human beings in Kalyuga. O Bhairava! Thy greatness is beyond the reach of mind and speech. Brahma and Vishnu have praised thee with great faith and devotion. O Beloved! Out of one thousand names, eight are dear to you. My salutations to you!

Hearing the above salutations from the sweet lips of his divine consort, Bhairava felt pleased.

> May that body of Immovable Shiva,
> Which is united with the beautiful body of Parvati:
> Remove misfortunes from this world.

One day, when the God and the Goddess were in a romantic mood, Shiva kissed the eyes of Parvati. Due to it, the lips and face of the Lord was covered with black *kajal*. Parvati feeling amused brought a mirror and placed it in front of her Lord. Seeing the patches of *kajal* on his face, Shiva laughed and hurriedly washed his face with waters of the Ganges. The Lord had brought the Ganges to Kashmir, for this purpose. Addressing Parvati, the Lord said:

> O Bhairavi! It is the same Ganges, which is known as Nila Ganga here in this blessed land. The Nila Ganga is the remover of all grave sins. On hearing story of the Nila Ganga, one attains the fruits of *Ashwa-mega-yaga*.
>
> With a dip in the pious water of the Nila Ganga, one is freed from all sins. Those pilgrims who apply sediment of the Nila Ganga on their bodies, would get rid of all worries and will feel peace within their souls. O Goddess! You are

worthy of worship even by the gods! In this way, I have related the great significance of the holy Nila Ganga. It is said that in Kalyuga, reading and listening the pious and mysterious story of the Nila Ganga would wash away all the terrible sins of human beings. Its greatness lies that it destroys even triple tragedies of the human beings.

Sathanwa Ashram

It is mentioned in the scriptures that for a long period, Parvati served her Lord, Shiva, at a place known as Sathanwa Ashram. The spot is very sacred, for it is here that Shiva performed his *Samadhi* for thousand of years. It is the Ashram of the Lord and many a devotees have had darshan of the Lord at this place.

The Lord related the story of Sathanwa Ashram as under:

O Bhairavi! O Goddess! Listen, now I am going to narrate the greatness of Sathanwa Ashram, known as Chandanwari. After listening to it one gets rid of one thousand great sins. In ancient times, after departure from Parvati, the Lord flew to the Himalayas and remained there in Mahasamadhi for a thousand years. To perform all services to her Lord, Parvati also appeared there and in many ways, served the Lord for a long period. At this place of Sathanwa Ashram, Lord Shiva observed a rigid penance. Therefore, this place is called as Sathanwa Ashram, which is destroyer of all evils and sins. O Goddess! Those pilgrims, who take bath near Sathanwa Ashram, become free from all worries and achieve great divine bliss. O Goddess! Those who offer different types of gifts to the Brahamans and the poor, according to Vedic injunctions, are blessed. By offering alms at this place, their fore-fathers become satisfied for decades.

The merits, which can be obtained from this pilgrimage are described by Shiva in the following words:

Both acute and ordinary sinners are liberated in the sacred forest of Sathanwa Ashram. Numerous results are obtained by performing the pilgrimage of Sathanwa Ashram, which is equivalent to as giving thousands of cows in charity. O Dear! By taking baths at Kurukshetra, Priyag and in the Ganges and Sangam, a man gets the same results as he gets by performing the pilgrimage of Sathanwa Ashram.

O Goddess! By offering cows, gold and silk garments and a *seer* of *Til* at Sathanwa Ashram, a man obtains a bundle of virtues. O Sundari! After taking a bath at the Tirtha, a man is free from all sins as a leaf of lotus in water.

O Parvati! The adorable body of your mother has been created by Brahama in the spotless family of the Pitrs. You are again and again on my lips which are engaged in murmuring salutations to you.

Bhairava continues describing attributes of Sathanwa Ashram in the following discourse:

O Dear! There a man should worship gods, offer water to his ancestors. By doing so, a man is sure to get rid of thousands of previous sins. O mother Goddess! One who does not have bath nor gives any thing in charity ows severe sins and is placed in hell. In ancient times, the Rakhasas along with the Devatas came to Sathanwa Ashram for darshan of God. O Maheshri! These people were uttering hymns first to me, and in the meantime, began to quarrel among each other; even they began to beat each other. O Beautiful! While climbing the mountains, the Devatas crushed the Rakhasas. After this all the demons were accumulated in the same mountain.

Pisu Bal

Pisu Bal or the Pisu hill is the stage between Nila Ganga and Sheshram Nag. It is sight of the fight, which occurred during ancient times, between the Devatas and the Rakhasas. When Shiva and Parvati had made the mountain as their abode, the Devatas wanted to have their darshan, but were stopped in the way by the devils. After the battle, the devils were crushed and ground down to pieces. *Pisna* means to grind down, and as such the etymology of the name Pisu Bal. The ascent to the hill is a little bit steep but the whole trouble of reaching the sumit is compensated by having a look on the grant panorama of forests and mountains.

O Bhairavi! After the defeat of the Rakhasas, this mountain was named as Pisu and became famous. On this mountain, the devotee crushes his sins. A man gets the same liberation and fruits by seeing Pisu as he gets by taking baths in Kurukshetra, Priyag and the Ganges. O Goddess! On Pisu hill, a man gets all those merits which he can obtain from *Bagh-payi-yuga* and sacred pilgrimage of *Namme Shariam*. On this mountain, a man gets thousand times better results than from *Kashi* and *Kurangagal*, and a lakh times better than *Mans Tirath*. O Goddess! A devotee who is desirous of climbing this mountain should chant the mantra: *Shri*, *Shri*, *Shri Shit Kontehesh* with acute love and concentrated mind. By doing this, one reaches that heavenly place where there is nothing to worry.

O Sati! O Gauri! O Parvati!
Salutations to you.
You alone can grant *mukti* to your devotees.
You alone can grant *siddhis* to your devotees.

When the Goddess heard her Lord, She replied:

O Lord! You are the Source.
O God! You are the Sustainer. Thou are the giver of everlasting bliss. I adore thee: Three-eyed-One! Please proceed with the story of Sri Amareshvara.

Bhairava felt pleased to hear sweet words from the sweet lips of his divine consort and said:

O Sundari! Salutations to you.
O Goddess! A man, who climbs this mountain as mentioned in *Shastras*, crushes his all sins and achieves the place of *Sadha Shiv* in this world without any hesitation. A man gets the highest place by seeing the Pisu. Side by side, all the enemies like *Dabeni* and *Shabeni* are smashed down in a moments time.

O Devi! Great are the merits of visiting the Pisu Tirtha.

O Goddess! Any one, who bows before the Pisu ascent with love and devotion, is connected with the supreme power: Brahma, without any trouble. Nothing more can be said on this subject as it is true without any doubt that in *Kalyuga*, any person by climbing Pisu hill, attains liberation and heavenly place. O Goddess! O Devi! I have narrated to you the sacred story of the Pisu ascent. This is the spot which is divine and sacred.

By only hearing, reading and chanting the name of Pisu, all sins of a man are crushed. O Beautiful! I have related to you this secret episode which gives result of *Ashmed-yuga*, if it is only heard, read and chanted.

The Lord again showered praises in honour of his consort in these words:

O Goddess! I adore your lotus-like eyes. You are sought after by self-less Yogis.
O Dearest! Your handsome smiling face gladens my heart.
Salutations to you again and again.
O Gauri! O Mother of the universe!
You are the other half of my body.

Sheshiram Nag

From Pisu mountain, the pilgrims have to travel to Zoj-pal, which is a beautiful camping ground. Adjacent to it is the sacred lake, known as Sheshiram Nag. It lies at the height of 11,730 ft. above the sea level, surrounded on one side by snow peaked mountains. The lake is fed by the waters of glaciers, and is sanctified as the lake in which, Parvati sails in a boat with her Divine Lover.

O Lord! Thou are the Moon.
O God! Thou are the Sun.
O Shiva! Thou are the Fire! Thou are the Air.
And thou are the Space.
O Bhairava! Thou are the Self.
O God! Thou are the Atman.

It so happened that a shop-keeper named Soda Wani lived near the Gopa hill and earned his living by selling candies. The shepherds used to obtain candies from him, while tending their flock on the Gopa hill. Every one would ask for one candy but one evening, one of the youngman, asked for two candies. On enquiry, he told Soda Wani that another youth comes to the hill along with his bull and the candy is for him. He also told that the youth rides the bull and goes beyond the mountains.

Soda Wani felt amazed to hear the strange story and desired to see the bull and the youth himself. He went to the spot and kept himself concealed in the bushes. What he saw was strange and curious. Suddenly, from above the mountains, a beautiful youngman came riding on a robust bull. In stead of flowers, the youth on the bull wore a garland of snakes. Soda Wani felt amazed, when the youngman started his dance; it appeared that the whole world danced with him at the rhythm of his feet. Now, he saw a beautiful young maiden approaching the youngman. It appeared that she was an apsara from the heaven and was a paragon of beauty. Both met and became one; then again, Soda Wani saw two persons and then again he felt that half of the body was of a man and the half was of a woman.

Both joined in an eternal embrace. It was a strange sight for Soda Wani, who wanted to know these young lovers. And when both of them rode on the bull and wanted to go, Soda Wani ran after them, caught hold of the tail of the bull.

The bull began to fly and Soda Wani cried: "Who are you, two lovers? Then youngman told him that they live at Sheshiram Nag and he can meet them here.

He is the Supreme Guru.
He manifests in all in varying degrees, and beyond the universe.
On his will there are no limitations.
From him emanates the light of liberation.
His countenance is benign.
He is the *Hamsah* himself.

On the Shiva-ratri, Soda Wani reached Sheshiram Nag. As

he could not find anyone, he waited alone calling for the youngman and the maiden. When evening approached, he felt dismayed and thought that both the lovers had deceived him. His sorrow and anger reached a high pitch. He did not cook anything nor ate anything. Before it was dark, he suddenly heared the sound of a *damroo*. He looked into the direction, when he saw the same lovers coming towards him on the back of a bull. Soda Wani felt happy thinking that the lovers had kept the promise. When they reached near him, the whole area engulfed itself into an aura of light. Both the lovers looked divine, majestic and sublime. Soda Wani felt puzzled but maintaining his courage, he asked again: "Who are you?" Suddenly, many gods surrounded the couple and after bowing before them recited as under:

Salutations to Thee! O Supreme Lord!
O God of gods! O Shiva, Bhairva, Mahadeva!
We prostrate ourselves before Thee.
O Goddess! O Sati, Uma, Parvati!
Salutations to Thee! O Devi!
O Divine Mother! We worship thee!

Hearing this, Soda Wani at once understood that the couple, whom he considered to be ordinary lovers were, no other than the Lord of the universe, Shiva and his beloved consort. He bowed and recited the following hymn in their honour:

O Lord of compassion!
Salutations to thee.
O Goddess! O Divine Mother!
Shower your blessings on me.
I bow before thee.
O Gauri, O Uma, O Shakti!
I worship your lotus feet.
O Shankara!
You have lead me from untruth to truth.
You have lead me from darkness to light.
Thou giver of boons!
Accept my salutations!

Saying this hymn, Soda Wani prostrated before the Lord and his consort. Shiva descended from the bull and holding hands of the devotee, picked him up. Granting him *vibhuti*, he said:

You are blessed!
You are granted liberation.
You will swim in the lake of nectar:
Sheshiram Nag!

Having said this, the divine beings disappeared in the clouds. Such is the story of the lake of Sheshiram, a dip into which washes away all sins.

The lake being so sacred, the divine consort, once asked her Lord as under:

O God! After hearing the significance and virtues of Pisu Gathi by your holy mouth, I am fully satisfied and pleased enough. O Bhairava! Now I want to hear the origin and familiarity of Sheshiram Nag.

O Lord! Be kind to relate the story of this lake to me.
O adorable Lord of compassion!
O Light of Lights!
O Shining One!
I live for Thee.
O adorable Lord of mercy and love!
Salutations to Thee.

Bhairava felt pleased to hear the above hymn from the sweet lips of his consort. Lovingly looking towards her, he said:

Bhairavi, Gauri, Uma, Parvati!
O Lotus-eyed! Your smiling face gladdens me.
O Light of Lights!
Thou are Infinite Beauty!
Thou are joy, bliss and peace.
O Goddess with thin waist.

O Gracious Consort! Now hear the story of the snake-headed Shesh-naga.
Let Indra speak for me.

Thus spoke Indra to Parvati:

Salutations to you, O Consort of the Lord. I will make you familiar with the sacred Tirtha of Sheshiram Nag, where all sins are crushed. During Satyuga, our Lord God, Shiva selected a place of worship, on the highest peak of the Himalayas, near Amareshvari. The place being sacred, all the gods came and resided there.

At the same time a proud demon was also residing there in the shape of air. He used to threaten all the assembled gods there. All the gods along with their king Indra, bowed at the feet of God, who was worshipping nearby, on Sampari. Finding them there, the Lord felt pleased and asked them the reason of their visit. They narrated their vows as under:

O God of all gods!
Salutations to Thee, our supreme Lord.
Thou are without beginning or end.
Thou are the creator, the preserver and the destroyer.
Thou are our father, mother and friend!
Thy greatness is beyond the reach of mind and speech.
Thou giver of refuge, Thou are the protector of the poor and the needy. Help us, our Lord God!

Hearing the prayers of the gods, Shiva began to talk in a sweet and melodious tone as under:

"O gods! I have heard every thing regarding this demon. Since I have created him, I cannot make an end of him. Therefore, you should seek the shelter of four armed Narayana. He is sleeping in the ocean on the head of Shesh Nag, holding *Gadha*, *Shank* and *Chakar*. Sending them off, Lord Shiva again went into a concentrated mind. Thereafter, all the gods, full with joy reached the ocean and began to pray to Vishnu, the feeder of the word, as follows:

O Protector of embryo, ocean of all virtues and knower of all good and bad acts. You are the Supreme reality underlying and pervading the whole universe. You are the ultimate cause of universe.
Being the Lord of all gods, you are known in the holy Vedas.
You are always busy in rescuing devotees from distress.

On hearing the prayers of gods, Lord Vishnu appeared before the Devatas and began to talk to them in a sweet and melodious tone. "You all go to my heaven without any delay and hesitation, I will make an end of that demon, who is in the shape of air, along with his family". After this, Lord Vishnu satisfied his devotees and went into a super concentration.

When Parvati had heard the above story, Shiva resumed it further in the following words:

Salutations to Thee, O Devi!
O Daughter of the Himalayas. Thereafter that four armed; the creator of world, along with Lakshmi; his consort; seated on *Shesh Nag*, appeared from *Patal*, the lower part of the universe. Thereafter, he ordered the *Saruf-raja*, the king of snakes, who is decorated with hundred heads to suck the air from the mountain, to destroy the unreached demon. After receiving orders, the *Saruf-raja* sucked the air from the mountain with his hundred mouths and thus killed the demon there, leaving no air in the mountain. From that date the snake also began to live in that dense mountain. Since then, the gods were freed and they live peacefully, without threat.

Then God addressed to Pavan Bakhi or the sucker of air: O you the king of snakes, stay here and crush all the calamities, which arise from air at this place. O Goddess! Since then, there dwells a snake named Shesh Nag. The great saints have named it Sukhsharan because all people are bestowed here with comforts or *sukh*. It is also called Swaashram because all gods got their respective Ashrams with the help of *Saruf-raja*. With its glimps all sinners are freed from their sins. By heaving glimpse of this place, or by taking a dip or by giving or by performing *Yagas*, a man attains liberation and is free from all sins. After this, a man should climb Mahagunus mountain, because by climbing this, a man has not to see the door of Yama.

Vavojana

The route to the sacred cave of Amarnatha passes through a high pass known as Vavojana, which is also termed as Vayuvarajana.[1] Since ancient times, the pilgrims to this place have added *maths* or stone huts for the Devas. Each pilgrim adds his stone and makes a shelter for the gods, because the wind blows very hard on this pass. It is considered a holy act to prepare a *math* or a hut at this place.

Then the Divine Consort asked the Lord:

O Bhairava! O Deva! I have heard the story of Sheshiram Nag. I want to hear regarding sacred Vavojana. O God! you had told me that small *maths* can be built there with good stones.

O Bhairava! Can human beings attain liberation by visiting this Tirtha? What merits are obtained by raising *maths* at this site?

The Lord of all gods asked Vishnu to relate the merits which are obtained from constructing *maths*, at the sacred site of Vavojana. Then said he:

O Devi! Listen, I am now going to relate to you the merits of these *Mathdans*, because there is no charity higher than this. O Daughter of the Himalayas! After constructing a math, with good and beautiful stones, it should be decorated with courtyards and all homely goods and

1. Kalhana; Rajatarangini, trans. Stein, Vol. II, p. 409

cloths. Then after offering Puja as mentioned in Shastras, with money and valuable goods, one should give this in charity to some Brahman. Those who have done this *Mathdana* shall be residing in Shiv Loka till there is existence of fourteen *Indras*. In the meanwhile, a demon named Preshat had come to know about the destruction of all demons at Pisu Gathi as per prayers of Devtas. He began to tease gods in the shape of air. The frightened and teased gods, in utter destitute condition obliged Shiva by chanting hymns in his honour.

"O Saviour of Devtas! Comfort giver, destroyer of all misfortunes. O! You being the endless, having no bottom, middle and end. We bow to you with grace. You being in the shape of Bhairava; Preventer of untimely deaths, decorated with moon at the head, we solemnly bow to you. You are calm, without any dirt, free of all wordly activities. We pray to you, O, you being the Amareshvara! We again and again bow to you with love and devotion."

When the Lords of the gods heard hymns sung in his praise, he felt pleased and satisfied.

Thou are the creator of universe.
Thou are the protector of world.
Thou are the destroyer of the cycle of births and deaths.
O Lord! O Great Magician!
With whatsoever faith or feeling we call on Thee, thou are pleased.
O Lord Mahadeva! Give us the knowledge and capacity to see the inner Soul.
Meditating on you alone, we do japa of *Lam*, *Vam*, *Ram*, *Yam*, *Ham*, *Om*!

As advised by Vishnu, the gods and the saints constructed small huts of stones at the site. Without any fear or threat, they began to live there peacefully and absorbed themselves in prayers. When they recited hymns, the demons kept quite. Their fury and anger cooled down.

> This is the incomparable and delightful abode of Vishnu. The excellent Yogi, at the time of death joyfully places his vital *Prana* here and enters that Supreme, Eternal, Birthless, Primeval Deva, the *Purusa*, who was before the three worlds, and who is known by the Vedanta.[1]

The Lord continues his discourse as follows:

But this demon showed his ugly shape again. Indra, seeing this huge and fearful shape, took some weapon and killed him on Vayuvarjana mountain. As due to this incident, the mountain was named as Vavojana. By taking a dip at Vayuvarjana and offering Puja and charities, a devotee attains great fame and is freed from his grave sins. It is quite true that those who do dot construct any ashrams at Vavojana are liable to be put in acute hell. One who will not give charities or will not take a dip here, his worship is baseless. O Goddess! Thus I have narrated the existence and origin of Vayuvarjana. By hearing, reading or listening this, one is freed from all sins.

Parvati then asked about Sushak-Sar, which is also known as Hukh-Sar, meaning the dried lake. The Lord replied that he will gladly relate the story of these dry lakes, so that her all doubts are cleared.

Some of the demons, who had saved themselves from destruction, concealed themselves in the ponds around Vavojana. After some time, they started teasing the gods and the saints. Once Shiva and his Consort were having a rendezvous, when Parvati told her Lord as under:

> O Lord! See the pitable condition of the gods and saints, who are being teased by the demons.
> Look at these gods, who are frightened.

Shiva took pity on the frightened gods and devotees. He blew his bugle so loud that the demons got scared and hid

---

1. Sat-Chakra-Nirupana, translation by Arthur Avalon

themselves in the ponds. Then Parvati cursed them, with the result that the ponds got dried up. The demons came out of the dried ponds but were killed by the gods. When the place was cleared of the demons, it became a fit place for habitation. Accordingly, the gods were directed to build stone huts as shelter against winds. Accordingly, the pilgrims to this place also build stone huts and obtain many merits.

The pilgrims who visit this place are advised to construct shelter huts of stones. At the same time, they are advised to pass from this place quietly without talking or uttering any word. Some of the demons may be still present at the place, hidden behind the stones.

Om!
Prostration to the Guru, who is Shiva.
Who is the embodiment of existence, knowledge, bliss and peace.
Thou are self-luminous.
Thou are Light-divine.
Thou are our father, mother, brother, friend, relative and Guru.

Panchatarangini

The high-level valley drained by the five sacred streams is known as the valley of Panchatarangini, popularly called Panchtarno. This place represents the plaited *Jata* of the Bhairava. Once the Divine Consort asked her Lord:

O Adorable Lord of Compassion!
Salutations unto thee. Please tell me about the sacred streams of Panchatarangini, on hearing of which, one gets liberation from births.

The Lord inclined to reply said:

O Devi! O Beautiful Goddess! I am relating the story of Panchatarangini, where taking a dip one gets as many benefits as he gets after performing *Ashvmed Yaga.* O High-souled Goddess! During ancient days at Tandav, while dancing, my *Jata*, the hair of head, spreaded into five parts. O Goddess! From the same five parts, the sacred Ganges began to flow, which washes away the severe sins of a man. O Maheshwari! This stream was named as Panchatarangini by the saints. By taking a bath at this place a man gets the same benefits and all other comforts as he get from taking a bath at Kurukshetra or Priyag. Any one, who gives in charity, gold, silk, chandan, safron and camphor attains Shiva Lok without any reason. Then he should climb the Rattan Shekhar peak and should go near Damrok, which is purely a devotee of Shiva in the shape of a stone. By its darshana one gets as many good wills and wishes fulfilled as he gets after performing *Ashvmed Yaga*.

Parvati was very much pleased to hear about the stages of the pilgrimage to Sri Amareshvara. The Lord had told her about the huge stone, known as Damrok, which represented him. Parvati wanted to know as to how Shiva manifested himself in the shape of a huge stone. In order to clarify, the Lord said as under:

O Maheshvari! O Bhairavi!
Now I tell you about Damrok and how it was shaped into a stone.
O Beloved! O Consort!
When I was busy dancing with my son, Kumara,
I forgot that the time of Sandhya was near.

Then the Lord said to Parvati:

O Beautiful! O Devi! Damrok is a Deva.
His duty was to awake me at the time of Sandhya.
One day, when I was playing with Kumara,
Damrok also joined in our play.
Accordingly, he forgot to remind me about the prayer time, with the result that the time of Sandhya passed away.
O Parvati! In rage I told Damrok as under:
" As you have failed to remind me about the time of Sandhya, you remain here in the shape of static stone."

O Goddess! From that day Damrok has served me in the shape of a stone. Any one who takes refuge on this stone will attain immortality.
After this, O Consort, it is necessary to proceed for Garbh Yatra.

After hearing the above, Bhairavi asked:

O Bhairava! O Deva! What is this Garbh Yatra?
Why it is there and what benefits a man gets after entering it?

The Lord replied as under:

O Goddess! Listen, I am narrating to you the importance of holy Garbh Yatra. After hearing to it one gets rid of all sins. In old days Devtas while discussing with each other came to Nandi.
In spite of his advice, they started to quarrel with each other, resulting in a war.
The gods showed their anger towards Nandi, who approached the Lord with the request to save him from the anger of the gods.

The Lord continued his discourse as under:

O Bhairavi! O Devi! O Consort!
After hearing Nandi, I told him:
"O Nandi! You lift this stick and Devtas will not harm you any more. You construct a Garb-ghar around yourself in the rock so that Devtas and even demons are not able to enter or come out of it. Nandi made a hole in a big rock, so that any one coming to him shall have to pass through this hole, which is Garbh-ghar. O Beloved! If any person enters the said holy Garbh-ghar, mixes with the heavenly Shiva Lok and he never comes again in the *Punar-janam*. Even after attaining the severe sain of murdering his father, mother, brother or any child, a man here gets rid of all his evils. O Goddess! If you also want to minimise

the sins of *Kalyug*, you also perform this Garbh Yatra. I take your oath and tell the truth that even the immoral soul will attain salvation by performing this Yatra. Thereafter one has to dip in the holy Amravati stream, apply *vibhuti* on his body and dressed in loin cloth only. Chanting the Mantra "O Shiva! show me the path", one has to worship Amareshvara, who is almighty.

CHAPTER III

Amareshvara Lingam

Everything is Shiva Lingam,
In the body,
As well as in the outer world;
Knowledge is Shiva Lingam.
Shiva is himself his own Lingam.

How Shiva manifested himself in the form of a Lingam is described in the Linga-Purana. Once conversation between Vishnu and Brahma developed into a dispute about their superiority. At that time an affulgent pillar of fire arose before their eyes. Brahma tried to find its top while Vishnu searched its bottom. But neither of them succeeded. As mystical sound of Om emanated from the pillar, they realised that it was the manifestation of Shiva.

Generally, representing the phallus of Lord Shiva, the Lingam can apply to several objects. The absolute form of Shiva is Alingam, while the visible form or manifestation is the Lingam. While Brahma is meant to represent the seed, Vishnu represents the Yoni, and Rudra is the cause of creation. All the three attributes mentioned above are combined in the Lingam, which is nothing else but Shiva. As such, everything in the cosmos is Shiva Lingam.

The materials used for Puja are, Madhuparka, Vasna, Abharana, Gandha, Pushpa, Dhupa, Navedya and Namaskarya.[1]

---

1. Madhuparka are the liquids like honey, milk, etc; Vasna is cloth;, Abharana jewels; Gandha perfumes, flowers; Dupa incense; Dipa lights Navedya food and Namaskarya prayers.

He who meditates upon this stainless Lotus.
Which is known as the Supreme Lingam,
Is freed immediately from all his enemies.
He becomes a lord among the Yogis.
He is like the sun, illuminating the darkness.

Parama Shiva is beyond the limits of time, space and form. He is eternal and his nature has a two-fold aspect as Shakti, he pervades the universe and as Shiva, he is beyond all universal manifestation. In fact, the cosmos, with all its variety of objects and means of experience, is nothing but a manifestation of the Shakti aspect of Parma-Shiva himself.[1]

He is the Supreme Self, absolute and indescribable One. He is omnipresent, omniscient and omnipotent. He is the Immortal.

The Divine Consort askes her Lord as under:

O Bhairava! O Maheshwara! I have heard the importance of all the Tirthas as Satisara, with joy and have crossed this ocean of *Janmas*. Now I want to hear the story of Amareshvara and how he got himself seated in the Amarnatha cave? How Amareshvara was formed and what benefits, a man gets from the Sangam of Amaravati?

Amaravati is known as the stream of immortality. When the gods approached Shiva to render them immortal, he rinsed his plaited *jata* and out of it emerged the Amaravati stream. Its water is amrit or the nectar of life.

In order to please his Consort, the Lord replied as follows:

O Bhairavi! O Worthy Goddess!
You have asked me this question for the benefit of people in this world. O Beautiful Goddess! I will narrate the sacred story of Amareshvara, on hearing which, one gets rid of all acute sins. O Ishvari! Prior to the origin of this universe, nothing was common or uncommon. At that time

1. Kashmir Shavism; pp. 44-45.

only God existed, who created all this universe. O Bhairavi! Your body is just like a full-bloomed flower. Your face is just like a full moon! Your gestures are all alluring! Black curls play on your forehead. What a panorama of beauty!

The Divine Consort reminded her Lord that she had asked a question about Amareshvara, while the Lord had started praising her beauty. Whereupon, the Lord informed the Divine Consort that she being the source of immortality, Amareshvara is immortal. Bhairava continues as under:

O Bhairavi! Parameshvara is the supreme Lord. Shiva is the Parama Shiva, which is in every thing and being in the universe. His manifestation is Shakti—that is you, O Devi! It is through you that I get light, bliss and joy. When you open yourself, the universe comes into being and when you close youself, the universe disappears. In fact you are the creator and it is through your kindness that *Aham* was born and after *Aham* my servants like Indra and others were created. Along with them, with the blessing of Paramal Shakti, all Rishis, Pitras, Gandarvas, Rakhasas, demons, devils, humans, animals and other creatures were born. In short, fourteen kinds of creatures having soul, were born at that time, due to Shakti-Tattava and Shiva-Tattva.

O Bhairavi! Then, Akasha, Vayu, Agni, Ap, and Prithivi were held together by me and you.

O Devi! Then the Death came and began to eat all *jivas*. O Consort! It is not liable to birth nor to death. It is not injured when it leaves the body of creatures. It is immortal but the body is mortal. Hence the *jiva* came and implored as under:

"O Parama Shiva! O Maheshvara!
You are omnipotent and omnipresent!
You are our creator, comforter and preserver!
We bow ourselves before you.
We continuously pray and worship you.

Thou are ageless and deathless!
But why Yama for the creatures like us.
O great Lord! Death eats everyone without any mercy.
Show us the way to be immortal."

It is the Atman, which is ageless, deathless, sorrowless, hungerless and fearless. That is Self or Parama Shiva and Parama Shakti. When the gods implored that the fear of death be removed from their hearts and Yama directed not to use force on them, Bhairava replied:

O Devtas! I am the creator and the destroyer!
Your Atman will not die!

Telling this, Shiva descended Chandarkala from his jata, so that all living beings render themselves immortal.

O Goddess! By descending Chandarkala, the stream of water which broke there is named as Amaravati.

O Bhairvai! The drops of Amrit which fell from the body of Shiva formed the shape of *vibhuti* after freezing. With the acute and intense love Shiva himself melted and Devas seeing this scene were much amused and began to worship him, singing hymns in sweet and melodious voice. Often that melted water again freezed and formed itself into Lingam. On seeing this the Devas repeatedly bowed and began to recite and chant. hymns.

"From today itself you become Amar and my this Lingam may become famous in all the three worlds."

All Devas after offering prayers and bowing to this Lingakar went to their respective homes after making a round of the holy Lingam.

Then the Lord continued as follows:

O Bhairavi! After giving this boon to the Devtas, the Lord seated himself in the Amarnatha cave. This cave is called the Amreshvara cave because the Mahadeva took off Chandarkala from his head for the benefit of Devas and all creatures to save them from the fear of approaching death. By having a darshan of Amareshvara, one can become fearless of Yama.

O Parvati! Recite the mantra of Amareshvara! Anyone who recites this mantra, becomes sinless and fearless. Salvation from death and birth lies in this mantra.

The mere utterance of the mantra is nothing but a movement of lips. In order to make the mantra work, one has to awaken it. Each man is Shiva and can attain the power of the Lord to the degree of his ability. Our two lips are Shiva and Shakti and their movement is the *maithuna* of the two. Whatever is heard in the form of sound is Shakti. She is the supreme speech and the supreme peace.[1]

The Lord continues telling Parvati as under:

O Goddess! For the sake of your love and devotion, I related this episode before you. While performing the pilgrimage, taking a dip in Amaravati and applying *vibhuti* on his body, one gets complete serenity and peace of mind. O Goddess! One who achieves pleasure in this cave by engaging himself in the Tandav dance, will be considered pious and equivalent to Rudra. O Goddess! Those pilgrims, who enter the cave without applying *vibhuti* on their bodies will suffer from disease and become a sinner for all the times to come. O Devi! Those who visit the holy cave of Amareshvara without full knowledge of pilgrimage will obtain little merit.

The Lord further says:

O Devi! Meditate on the Guru in the lotus of a thousand petals, which is radiant like the cool rays of the full moon. O Beloved! Meditate on the Guru, whose lotus hands make the gestures which grant blessing and dispel fear. O Bhairavi! Meditate on the Guru, who is sitting in the Holy Cave of Amareshvara.

1. John Woodroff, The Serpent Power, pp. 96-101.

O Goddess! One who enters the Cave without performing *Tandav* dance, betrays the holy place of Sri Amareshvara. One who returns without worshipping the Shiva Lingam will be liable for the hell. One who returns without bestowing any charities at the Cave will go to the hell named as Kalsotara. O Beautiful! A person with acute sin or anybody having wild sins, will attain salvation and get rid from all sins, if he worships at the sacred abode of Bhairava.

O Devi! Here dwells the Lord!
Here flow the drops of nectar, resembling the silvery beam of the moon.
Bhairava tells about the merits obtained by the devotees, who pay a pilgrimage at the sacred Tirtha of Sri Amareshvara, in the following words:

O Beauteous one! O Shakti!
Sri Amareshvara is the abode of God:
It is the refuge of the refugeless!
It is the refuge of the sinners!
Even murderers, drunkards, killers of cows, and worst offenders can get rid of all their sins, by performing the pilgrimage of Sri Amareshvara.
Within this cave are the gods and the goddesses.
Within it, is Brahma, the creator, Vishnu, the preserver, Shiva, the destroyer, and above all Shakti, the daughter of the Himalayas.

Amareshvara Lingam

In the north-eastern side of the cave, there exists the self-created immortal Lingam of pure greenish ice, which waxes and wanes according to the phases of the moon.

Parama-Shiva is the Shiva-Linga!
The Universe is the manifestation of this Linga.
O Sundari! O Devi! O Uma!
This Lingam is the eternal truth.
Its darshan will save the liars.
Its darshan is more meritorious than fasts.

O Bhairavi! O Parvati! O Consort!
It is Sidhi-Lingam!
It is Buddhi-Lingam!
It is Sudhi-Lingam!

Since ancient times, this Lingam of Shiva has benefited human beings. It has given solace, contentment and bliss to the devotees. It is the harbinger of happiness, health, prosperity and long life. It is the refuge of sinners as well as saints. It is the refuge of all Yogis and all Yogins.

Then the Lord addressed his Consort in these words:

O Consort! O Bhairavi! O Parvati!
O Goddess! If you desire to achieve eternal salvation without meditation and offering any kind of charities, you should take refuge in the holy Amareshvara. All human beings should treat worldly things as futile and should worship Amareshvara.
O Mother of the Universe! O Kundalini!
Every one, should worship thee in Amareshvara!

All the Tiraths in the world are not even equal to the Tirtha of Amareshvara. O Maheshwari! In reality, all persons in Kalyuga are wraped in the wordly affairs and suffer a lot, even having the holy Amareshvara cave at their disposal. Not to speak repeatedly, it is quiet apparent that all those performing the pilgrimage will be freed from all sins.

Salutations to Sati in whom Rajas preponderates for the creation of this world.

Salutations to Uma in whom Tamas preponderates for the preservation of this world.

Salutations to Parvati in whom Sattva preponderates for giving happiness to the people of this world.

Shiva and Parvati

The Kashmiris believe that after his marriage, Shiva stayed in this sacred cave along with his divine spouse, Parvati. As such, the cave of Amareshvara is the abode of the Lord. At the time of darshana, two pigeons make their appearance and fly from their perches. Seeing these birds, the pilgrims clap their hands in joy having seen the Lord and his consort. These pigeons are the manifestation of the God and the Goddess. Bhairavi asks from the Lord:

> O Bhairava! O Lord! Who are these Shiv Gans in the form of pigeons and why they reside in the holy cave? Shiva! O God! Please describe the whole story for the benefit of the devotees.

Bhairava gave the following reply to the question of Parvati:

> O Vishnu! Salutations to thee!
> You give happiness to the people.
> Please relate the story of Ganas to Parvati.
>
> In compliance to the wishes of the God of gods, Vishnu addresses the Goddess as under:
>
> Salutations to thee, O Divine Mother!
> Thy Divinity is eternal. I offer my hymns.
>
> O Parvati! O Devi! Listen, I will tell you who were these pigeons and why they live in the cave. On the same day when Lord Shiva cursed his chief servant Damrok, other servants were selected in his place to alert Lord Shiva for Sandhya. One day when Lord Shiva was dancing during Sandhya time, the selected Gans full with inner joy told to each other: "*Kuro, Kuro*", meaning "do the same dance". Then Lord Shiva cursed the servants for not alerting him at Sandhya time with the blessing: you will remain in the Amareshvara Cave for a long time and will chant the word *Kuro, Kuro*. Lord blessed them and bestowed them with the power of removing all misfortunes and obstacles of all pilgrims to the abode of Shiva. O Goddess! By the words of high powered Lord Shiva, they assumed the form of pigeons and started to relieve the pilgrims of their misfortunes. O Dear! Those people who return back without seeing these pigeons on this mountain are called by holy persons not to

have completed the darshan. Therefore, all should try to have darshana of these pigeons to satisfy their desires. The holy saints call them *Path Darshan* or shower of Paths and destroyer of all sins.

There is no God better than Shiva. There is no hymn better than the hymn on the greatness of Shiva. There is no sacred word better than the name of Shiva.

Salutations to the God of gods.
Salutations to thee, O Goddess.

Parvati felt pleased to hear the story of the pigeons. But she had other questions in mind and wanted her Lord to tell her more about other matters. She addressed her Lord in the following words:

O Lord! The fury of thee who became a hunter with a bow in hand has not as yet left Brahma though, keenly pierced by thy arrow and terror stricken, he has fled to the skies.
O Three-eyed One! You are kind to the devotees.
You have allowed me to occupy half of thy body.
O Destroyer of Tripura! I bow to you.
With trishul in your hand, you grant boons to the devotees. You fulfil their desires and give them treasures, which they enjoy. I bow to you.
You have pleased me by relating the sacred story of Amareshvara. My salutations to thee, O my Lord.

Bhairavi here speaks of the greatness of Shiva. There is no limit to the greatness of the Lord, for even Brahma and other gods are not fully aware of his greatness. His greatness is beyond the reach of mind and speech.

Bhairavi asks the following question:

O Bhairava! O Deva!
Which is the suitable and beneficial time for darshan, chanting of hymns or performing of pilgrimage of Sri Amareshvara? O Giver of refuge!
What results will sinners get by taking a dip in the streams of Amravati and Panchtarni?

O God! Relate the benefits of pilgrimage to the Tirtha of Sri Amareshvara?

After hearing the above, the Lord replied as follows:

O Consort! Even the gods are ignorant of the extent of thy greatness. The praises of all gods are inadequate for thee. O Devi! You are the pool of nectar!

O Goddess! You are the sincerest devotee of Sri Amareshvara. It is most beneficial and worthy of merits, to have the darshana of Sri Amareshvara on *Sawana Purnamashi*.

It is essential that all pilgrims must worship the Shiva Lingam at the tirtha of Sri Amareshvara on *Purnamashi*, the full moon of the month of Sawana. Having no consciousness of physical world, the sincere devotees, both male and female will discard worldly cloths, before they would enter the sacred cave.[1] Sri Amareshvara is the eternal and immortal emblem of Shiva. The Lord has himself related its merits in the following words:

O Beautiful One! Everything is Shiva Lingam!
Shiva is himself his own Lingam.
Amareshvara is the immortal Lingam of Siva.
By touching the Holy Lingam, a devotee achieves salvation.
One should, therefore, offer flowers to the Lingam and obtain merits.

O Bhairavi! O Light of Lights!
An Adorable One! Thou are Infinite Beauty!
It is true that a devotee obtains great fruits of Yoga, by worshipping the Amareshvara Lingam.
Those who pass round the Holy Lingam, with a vessel of water, obtain bliss.
Those who offer scent, *dhoop*, ghee lamps, camphor, fruits and flowers to the holy Amareshvara Lingam, obtain freedom from all sorrow and misfortunes of life. Let sixty-four lamps be lighted around the Lingam of Siva.

1. Lawrence; The Valley of Kashmir: "It is customary with the devotees of Shiva to enter the cave naked and dance around the holy Lingam but this custom is not adhered to by non-Shaivites."

O Beautiful Goddess! O Parmeshvari! Making rounds of the Lingam at Amareshvara obtains the same merits, which one obtains from performing *Ashmeda-Yaga.*

Amareshvara Cave is the abode of Shiva, which is free from *Maya.* It is replete with every form of bliss and in it dwells the Creator, Destroyer and Preserver of the three worlds. Mahadeva who is the Lord of all, has manifested himself here in the shape of Svayambhu-Lingam, which is radiant like the cool rays of the full moon. This is Itara-Shiva in ice crystal, from which flows the stream of nectar.

O Devi! Meditate on this Maha-Lingam Svayambhu.
Meditate upon Syama, who surrounds this Lingam.
Salutations to the region of Fire with his ten *Kalas.*
Meditate upon Sada-Gauri, who is the other half of the body of Shiva.
Meditate upon the Lingam-Itara, with three eyes.
Meditate on His form which includes all the four Gurus.
He who is the Lord of all, is Parama-Shiva.
Amareshvara is the abode of Shiva:
The Shaivites call it as such.
The Vaishnavites call it the place of Vishnu.
Others call it the place of Hari-Harra.
But the sages call it the place of Shakti-Shiva.

O Parvati! All the gods and their consorts offer homage to thee. You are life of all that lives.

Epilogue

The immortal cave of Sri Amareshvara, known as Srī Amar Nath Ji, situated amidst snow-bound mountains at a height of 12,729 feet above sea level, is invested with many sacred associations. The self-made ice Lingam of Lord Shiva perched on a glacial gorge is an interesting phenomenon. The waxing and waning of the Lingam with the moon has remained a world mystery. According to the common belief it reaches the maximum height on the *Puranmashi* (full moon) on Sawan, which is the day of pilgrimage. On this day thousands of pilgrims negotiate the spur leading to the sacred cave for darshan. The glacial gorge in the sylvan setting is a breath-taking sight indeed.

The pilgrimage provides adventure and spiritual solace. The journey lies through the most picturesque mountains in the world.

The cave is situated at a distance of 142 kms. from Srinagar. The first 96 kms. up to Pahalgam are motorable and the remaining 46 kms. are covered on foot on ponies.

Chandanwari : Altitude 9,500 feet.

Distance : 14 kms. from Pahalgam.

A small Shut-up valley at the junction of the streams from Sheshnag and Astanmarg. This is the first stage of the Yatra.

Sheshnag : Altitude 12,200 feet.

Distance : 13 kms. from Chandanwari.

Here the ascent is steep upto Pisu Top. After trudging along a spur for 5 kms. Sheshnag is reached. A dip into the ice-cold waters of the lake washes away the sins, according to common belief. Wavjan is a nice camping ground. This is the second stage of the yatra on way to the holy cave.

Panchtarni : Altitude : 12,000 feet.

Distance : 13 kms. from Sheshnag.

On way the Pilgrims cross the five rivulets at the foot of the mountain. The route begins with a stiff uphill climb to Mahagunus top (the great Viper) which commands a height of 14,000 feet. Then it winds down to the plain meadow of Panchtarni. This is the third and last stage of yatra.

From Panchtarni, the cave at an altitude of 12,729 feet is 6 kms. away. It is a short uphill route. Going round the spur one comes to a spot known as Sangam where Amravati stream joins the waters of Panchtarni. Covering an ascent of 3 kms. from here, the pilgrims reach the cave to pay homage to the Lord Shiva.

The route to Amarnathji remains open from August. The *Chari Mubarik* will leave Pahalgam for Chandanwari on the early morning of mid-August.

For the facility of pilgrims, the Government makes arrangements for providing transport provisions, shelter, firewood, medical aid, etc. For arranging ponies and porters as well as registration, etc., a base camp at Nun Wan (near Pahalgam) is set up during yatra.

To enable the State Government to handle the onrush of pilgrims with maximum speed and efficiency, all pilgrims-*cum*-tourists are requested to send intimation regarding their requirements of riding ponies/pack ponies/dandies/pithoo/mazdoors to the Tourist Officer, Pahalgam by 15th August.

The following arrangements are being made by the Government:

Transport

(*i*) For pilgrims adequate number of direct buses to Pahalgam will be made available at Pathankot/Jammu/Srinagar.

(*ii*) Riding and pack ponies, dandies, mazdoors and pithoos will be available at Pahalgam at fixed rates.

Accommodation

Tented accommodation with requisite furniture, etc., will be available at controlled rates at Pahalgam. You can make advance reservation for tents pitched at Chandanwari, Sheshnag and Panchtarni on payment with the Department of Tourism, at Pahalgam.

First Aid

A Medical Unit will cater to the needs of Yatries free of charges at all stages. Doctors, male and female, nurses, compounders, bearers and dais will accompany the yatra.

Cafeteria

Arrangement of a mobile cafeteria to accompany the yatra for the facility of pilgrims-*cum*-tourists, during the yatra from Pahalgam to Amarnath and back will have been made. Yatries can have food, tea, coffee, etc., at fixed rates.

Drinking Water

Drinking water drums and tanks fitted with taps shall be provided at steep and arduous places. Yatries are advised not to use this water for washing of cloths.

Camp Office at Nunwan Pahalgam

The Camp Office at Nunwan (Pahalgam) starts functioning from August and will remain open till the yatra ends.

Food Rations

Food ration depots will be established at various stations of the yatra for supplies of foodstuff such as rice, atta, kerosene oil, salt, sugar, dry milk, etc., to the pilgrims. The depots will mainly be stationed at

(*i*) Chandanwari.
(*ii*) Sheshnag.
(*iii*) Panchtarni.

Fuel (Firewood)

(*i*) Chandanwari.

(ii) Pisu Top.
(iii) Sheshnag.
(iv) Wavjan.
(v) Waybal.
(vi) Mahagunus.
(vii) Panchtarni.
(viii) Cave.

Travel Notes

The following information has been provided by M/s. Trans-Himalayan Travel and Tours, 15 Poloview, Residency Road, Srinagar, Kashmir, India.

Tourists-*cum*-pilgrims are advised, in their own interest to get in touch with any Travel Agent for making necessary arrangements for this trip to the Holy cave of Sri Amar Nath Ji. The following facilities are available:

(*a*) Riding ponies and pack ponies are available from Pahalgam to the Tirtha and back, at reasonable rates.

(*b*) Mazdoors and labourers are available for carriage of bedding, tents and quipment.

(*c*) Planquins and dandies are available for carriage of old, aged and infirm.

(*d*) Guides are available for trekking.

(*e*) It is necessary to get your reservation confirmed in advance.

(*f*) Tents, furniture, utensils, camp beds, cooking equipment and other travel equipment is available on rent.

M/s Trans-Himalayan Travel and Tours, 15 Poloview, Residency Road, Srinagar, Kashmir, India, have supplied the following itinerary:

Day	*Distance*	*From*	*To*
First	16 km.	Pahalgam	Chandanwari
Second	12 km.	Chandanwari	Sheshnag
Third	13 km.	Sheshnag	Panjtarni
Fourth	6 km.	Panjtarni	Sri Amar Nath Cave
Fifth	6 km.	Holy Cave	Panjtarni

Sixth	13 km.	Panjtarni	Wavjan
Seventh	12 km.	Wavjan	Chandanwari
Eighth	16 km.	Chandanwari	Pahalgham

Instructions

1. It is better to join the Yatra and visit the holy cave in the company of other pilgrims.

2. Carry your own equipment, such as, tents, warm clothing, woollens, rain-coats, torches, walking sticks, etc., with self.

3. Do not eat raw fruit during your journey.

4. Do not drink water from the ponds, springs and streams until it is boiled. It is better to have tea or coffee instead.

5. Do not try to overtake others, rather keep on walking slowly, so as to acclimatize yourself to high altitude.

6. Please carry your food, cooking equipment, medicines, etc., along with you, and do not depend upon others.

7. Do not carry arms or ammunition, nor kill any bird or animal.

8. You are advised not to sell your equipment, nor purchase any curio, work of art, statue and antiquity, which is more than hundred years old.

9. Please do not purchase herbs or medical remedies on the road-side.

10. In case of difficulty, always consult the local officers of the Government.

Travellers Equipment List

Personal	*Cooking equipment*
Sleeping bag	Oil stove
Ruek-sak	Kerosene oil
Jackets	Matches
Gloves	Pots and panes
Stocks	Small jug
Rubber-sole shoes	Tumbler

Toilet paper
Paper and diary
Ball point pens
Pencils
Shaving blade and shaver
Tooth paste and brush
Face cream
Vaseline
Goggles
Needle and thread
Handkerchiefs
Cap
Torch
Mirror
Comb
Hair cream
Talcum Powder
Soap

Food

Condensed milk
Tea
Coffee
Sugar
Tin fish
Tin meat
Tin vegetables
Biscuits
Instant soup
Alcoholic drinks

Photographic equipment
Camera with flash
Film reels
Camera stand
Equipment bag
Binocular

Medicines

Tourists are advised to carry high-altitude medicinal remedies with them for head-ache, nose-bleeding, fever, lose-motion, bad-cold, vomiting, travel sickness, eye trouble and muscle and back-ache.

Other Routes

Tourists, pilgrims and trekkers use two other routes also which are described as under:

(*a*) *Sonamarg route*: Srinagar to Sonamarg, Sonamarg to Baltal, Baltal to Sangam, Sangam to Sri Amar Nath Cave. From Srinagar to Sonamarg and Baltal, vehicles, cars and buses are available. From Baltal, one has to trek to the Holy Cave, which is only 16 km. from Baltal. As such, the pilgrimage takes only one day.

(*b*) *Astanmarg route*: Pahalgham to Chandanwari; Chandanwari to Astanmarg, Astanmarg to Sashkuti to Hatyara, Hatyara to Posh-Pathri, Posh-Pathri to Kel-Nar, Kel-Nar to Nagar-Pal, Nagar-Pal to Panjtarni, Panjtarni to Sri Amar Nath Ji.

Bibliography

M.A. Stein, *Ancient Geography of Kashmir* (English)

Aziz Ahmad Qureshi, *Asrar-i-Kasheer* (Urdu)

Ram Chandra Kak, *Ancient Monuments of Kashmir* (English)

Anand Koul Bamzai, *Archaeological Monuments in Kashmir* (English)

F.M. Hassnain, *Buddhist Kashmir* (English)

J.N. Ganhar and P.N. Ganhar, *Buddhism in Kashmir and Ladakh* (*English*)

Jean Naudou, *Buddhists of Kashmir* (English)

Bagvad-gita (Sanskrit)

Birihan-Nila-Tantram (Sanskrit)

Bodha-Pancha-Desha, (Sanskrit)

Devinam-villas (Sanskrit)

J.C. Chatterji, *Hindu Realism* (English)

F.M. Hassnain, *Hindu Kashmir* (English)

Hari-Har-Satotra (Sanskrit)

P.N.K. Bamzai, *History of Kashmir* (English)

Sarla Khosla, *History of Buddhism in Kashmir* (English)

Edit. F.M. Hassnain, *Heritage of Kashmir* (English)

Ishvara-Pratyabhijna (Sanskrit)

Edit: Barret, *Kashmirian Atharva-Veda* (English—Sanskrit)

Jagdish Chandra Chatterji, *Kashmir Shaivism* (English)

Ghulam Sarwar, *Khazinat-ul-Asfiya* (Urdu)

G.M.D. Sufi, *Kasheer* (English)

Loka-Prakasha (Sanskrit)

Laugakshi-Grhya-Sutra (Sanskrit)

BIBLIOGRAPHY

Lallashawari—Vakayani (Sanskrit)

Anand Koul, *Lalleshwari* (English)

Mohamad Din Fauq, *Lalla Arifa* (Urdu)

George Grierson and Barnett, *Lalla Vakyani* (English)

Mohamad Amin Pandit, *Ladakh-Ki-Kahani* (Urdu)

F.M. Hassnain, Masato Oki and Tokan Sumi, *Ladakh—The Moonland* (English)

Mahayana-Prakasha (Sanskrit)

Malini-Vijaya-Vartikam (Sanskrit)

Mregenda-Tantram (Sanskrit)

Birbal Kachru, *Majmooha-at-Tawarikh* (Persian)

Mohamad Ali, *Mirat-us-Safa* (Persian)

Faiz-ul-Haq-Hussaini, *Manshoor-i-Saadat* (Persian Manuscript)

Edit. and Trans. Ved Ghai, *Nila-Mata-Purana* (English and Sanskrit)

Mohamad Amin Kamil, *Noor-Nama* (Kashmir)

Netra-Tantram (Sanskrit)

Pratyabhijna Hrdeyam (Sanskrit)

Paramartha-Sara (Sanskrit)

Panchastavi (Sanskrit)

Shivnath Sharma, *Roopa-Bhavani* (Hindi)

Trans. M.A. Stein, *Rajatarangini* (English)

Edit. Srikanth Koul, *Rajatarangini* (Sanskrit—English)

Shiv-Sutra-Vimarshini (Sanskrit)

Varada Raja, *Shiv-Sutra-Vartikam* (Sanskrit)

Shiv-Drishti (Sanskrit)

Abdul Wahab, *Shahnama Kashmir* (*Persian*)

Shms-Faqir (Kashmiri)

Svacchanda-Tantram (Sanskrit)

Trans. Rati Ram Sharma, *Shiva-Maha-Purana* (Urdu)

V.N. Hoon, *Symphony of Bhagavad-Gita* (English)

Pavitrananda, *Shiva-Mahimnah-Stotram* (English)

S.L. Vaishnavi, *Shiv-Linga* (English)

Edit: Nila Kanth Gurtoo, Dina Nath Yaccha and Kashi Nath Handoo, *Sri Amareshwara Darshanam* (Hindi)

Rugh Nath Dhar, *Sawanih-Hayat-i-Roopa Bhawani* (Urdu)

A.Q. Rafiqi, *Sufism in Kashmir* (English)

Ghulam Rasul Wani, *Shams-ul-arifeen* (Urdu)

Dilbar Kashmiri, *Salikan-i-Kashmir* (Urdu)

Hassan Shah Kuehami Edit. and trans. Mohamad Ibrahim, *Tarikh-i-Aulia-i-Kashmir* (Urdu—Persian)

Mohamad Din Fauq, *Tarikh-i-Aqwami-Kashmir* (Urdu)

Hassan Shah Kuehami, *Tarikh-i-Kashmir* (Persian)

Syed Ali, *Tarikh-i-Kashmir* (Persian)

Narayan Koul Aajiz, *Tarikh-i-Kashmir* (Persian)

Edit. A.T. Hingorani, *Teachings of the Gita* (English)

Udamar-eshwarnantram (Sanskrit)

Vijnava Bhairava (Sanskrit)

Walter Lawrence, *Valley of Kashmir* (English)

Mohamad Azam, *Waqia-i-Kashmir* (Persian)

R.C. Temple, *Words of Lalla—The Prophetess* (English)

The Amareshvara ice Lingam inside the Holy Cave

Human-faced Shiva Lingam-Stone, Kashmir. 9th Century

Pilgrims proceeding to the Holy Cave